*For those who continue to search for what reality is—
and what it means to be part of it.*

REALITY AS A MULTI-DIMENSIONAL CAUSATIONAL FIELD

An Ontology of Structure, Meaning, and Participation

JOHN R. CARLOS

Published by Rondelet Press
- Houston, TX

ISBN 978-1-967386-57-4 (Softcover Book)
ISBN 978-1-967386-59-8 (eBook)

Printed in
First Edition.

"We are participators in bringing into being not only the near and here but the far away and long ago."

—John Archibald Wheeler

TABLE OF CONTENTS

Part II — The Multi-Dimensional Causational Model

Part III — Consciousness, the Soul, and Participatory Reality

Part IV — Meaning, Agency, And Civilizational Futures

Part V — Synthesis And Implications

Appendices

AUTHOR'S DECLARATION

This monograph represents my own intellectual work. It is an original synthesis of ideas developed through my ongoing research and reflection, grounded upon the scholarship of the many thinkers and disciplines I have acknowledged throughout the text. While it draws upon established scientific, philosophical, and metaphysical traditions, the conceptual model, interpretations, and arguments presented here are, to the best of my knowledge, my own and have not been copied or derived from any other author's work. This monograph is offered as an independent contribution to the study of reality, agency, and participation.

PREFACE

This monograph develops a multi-dimensional causational model of reality—an ontological framework that brings together physical structure, metaphysical meaning, temporal asymmetry, and quantum informational potentiality. Its central claim is that reality is not merely a passive environment in which events unfold, but a participatory field shaped by the interplay of structure, agency, and consciousness.

The ideas presented here did not emerge in isolation. They form part of a broader intellectual project that spans speculative fiction, philosophical inquiry, and civilizational analysis. Much of the conceptual scaffolding of this model first took shape during my work on the science-fiction novel ***Cryonic Dreams: Awakening***, where I explored how small shifts in meaning, agency, and interior life can cascade into large-scale civilizational trajectories. That fictional experiment prompted a deeper investigation into the underlying dynamics that govern human behaviour, institutional coherence, cultural fragmentation, and the emergence of possible futures.

Parallel to this creative work, a series of philosophical essays examining civilizational meaning collapse and renewal helped refine the questions that guide this monograph: How do physical, metaphysical, temporal, and informational dimensions interact to shape what becomes actual? What role does consciousness play in selecting among potential futures? And how do individuals and civilizations preserve coherence amid entropic and interpretive drift?

While those broader explorations form the backdrop to this project, the present work is focused on a single task: to articulate a coherent ontology of reality as a **multi-dimensional causational field**. The aim is neither to resolve scientific debates nor to advance testable physical theories, but to provide a conceptual model capable of integrating structural, experiential, and participatory dimensions of existence.

Readers will encounter here an attempt to synthesize insights from physics, information theory, metaphysics, and consciousness studies into a unified account of how reality becomes real. The model is necessarily speculative in parts, but its purpose is not prediction—it is clarification. It seeks to illuminate how agency, meaning, and consciousness interact with the deeper structures of the universe and how these interactions shape not only individual experience but the futures available to civilizations.

In this framework, the human person is not a linear or closed system but a **recursive participatory agent**. Every act of agency crosses the reality interface, actualising potential into consequence, and every consequence returns as experience, requiring reinterpretation and reintegration. Identity, consciousness, meaning, and agency therefore form a self-correcting causational circuit rather than a terminal chain of effects.

If this monograph contributes in any way to understanding the layered nature of causation—or to recognising that human participation has ontological weight—then it has fulfilled its intended purpose. It stands as one component of a larger inquiry, but it is self-contained in its scope: a philosophical and conceptual exploration of reality as an emergent, structured, and participatory field.

John R. Carlos
Canberra, Australia
2026

ACKNOWLEDGEMENTS

This work would not have been possible without the many thinkers, teachers, and companions whose insights have shaped my understanding of reality and the human place within it. I am indebted to those whose intellectual traditions form the foundation of this model—philosophers, physicists, theologians, and scholars across disciplines who dared to ask questions that resist simple answers.

Above all, I am grateful to those who continue the perennial search for understanding, whose curiosity and courage keep alive humanity's oldest question: *What is reality?*

PART I

-

FOUNDATIONS OF REALITY

CHAPTER 1

INTRODUCTION

1.1 The Central Question

Few questions have endured across the history of human thought as persistently as the inquiry, *What is reality?* From Plato's ideal forms to the probabilistic frameworks of modern quantum mechanics, thinkers have wrestled with whether reality is a mind-independent structure or a phenomenon inseparable from consciousness. The long arc of philosophical and scientific reflection reveals a tension between two intuitions: that reality exists "out there," independent of us, and that reality is somehow shaped, mediated, or even brought forth through perception and participation.

This book advances that ancient inquiry by proposing a **Multi-Dimensional Causational Model of Reality**—a framework that integrates the physical, metaphysical, temporal, and quantum aspects of existence into a single, coherent ontology. Yet such a model cannot be complete without addressing the persistent gap in scientific accounts: the nature and role of consciousness. The model therefore incorporates **consciousness—and by extension, the soul phenomenon—as the participatory dimension of reality**, the element that bridges potentiality and actuality.

1.2 Historical and Philosophical Context

Philosophical debates about the nature of reality form a lineage of competing metaphysical commitments. Realist traditions hold that the universe exists independently of our perceptions and that scientific inquiry uncovers truths about this pre-existing structure.[1] Idealist perspectives, conversely, argue that reality is fundamentally mental or immaterial, shaped by consciousness or mediated through perceptual frameworks.[2] Between these poles lies a spectrum of positions, from dualism to contemporary physicalism and anti-realism, each offering different responses to the ontological and epistemological puzzles at stake.[3]

Modern physics complicates these long-standing

[1] Psillos, S. *Scientific Realism: How Science Tracks Truth*. Routledge, 1999

[2] Berkeley, G. *A Treatise Concerning the Principles of Human Knowledge*. 1710

[3] Heidegger, M. *Being and Time*. Harper & Row, 1962

dichotomies. Quantum mechanics disrupts classical determinism, revealing a world in which indeterminacy, superposition, and the observer effect challenge assumptions about objectivity and causation. Cosmology likewise reframes the question of reality within a universe evolving under entropy, expansion, and deep temporal asymmetries.[1 2] These scientific developments demand a conceptual framework capable of integrating physical structure, information, and experiential participation into a unified account.

1.3 Scientific Foundations and Limitations

Science approaches reality through empiricism—the disciplined practice of observation, experimentation, and falsifiability—which has yielded some of humanity's most powerful and reliable knowledge.[3] Yet empiricism rests on methodological constraints that limit its explanatory scope. Physicalist models, which reduce all phenomena to matter and energy, struggle to fully account for subjective experience, agency, and

[1] Wheeler, J. A. "Law Without Law." In *Quantum Theory and Measurement*, Princeton University Press, 1983

[2] Penrose, R. *The Road to Reality*. Vintage, 2005

[3] Popper, K. *The Logic of Scientific Discovery*. Routledge, 1959

the participatory role of observation implied by quantum theory.[1 2]

This gap between third-person description and first-person experience—the so-called "hard problem" of consciousness—remains unresolved. It is precisely this explanatory absence that motivates the present model. Any adequate ontology of reality must address not only the structural components of the universe but also the experiential and participatory dimensions through which those structures become meaningful and actual.

1.4 The Proposed Solution

To address these challenges, this monograph introduces a **multi-dimensional causational model** consisting of four interrelated dimensions:

- **Physical Reality:** The domain of matter, energy, and space.
- **Metaphysical Reality:** The domain of social, cultural, symbolic, and environmental constructs.
- **Temporal Reality:** The irreversible flow of

[1] Hameroff, S., & Penrose, R. "Consciousness in the Universe: A Review of the Orch-OR Theory." *Physics of Life Reviews*, 2014

[2] Wigner, E. P. "Remarks on the Mind-Body Question." In *Symmetries and Reflections*, Indiana University Press, 1967

time driven by entropy and oriented toward causational end states.

- **Quantum Substrate:** The informational layer of coherence, entanglement, and probabilistic potentiality.

These dimensions provide a structural and informational account of the universe. Yet even taken together, they remain insufficient unless the **participatory dimension of consciousness** is included. In this model, consciousness is not merely an emergent by-product of neural complexity but an active participant in the formation of actuality. It interfaces with the quantum substrate, collapsing potentiality into concrete states and generating coherence across the experiential continuum. The **soul phenomenon**, conceptualised here as a quantum-informational substrate, provides continuity, agency, and unity across time—completing the model by embedding consciousness within the fabric of causation.

Importantly, this participatory act is not terminal. Every actualised outcome returns through the same interface as lived consequence, entering consciousness as experience. That experience revises meaning, recalibrates identity, and reshapes subsequent agency, rendering participation inherently recursive.

Together, these layers transform reality from a passive structure to a **co-created continuum**, shaped by the interplay of physical forces, metaphysical constructs, temporal constraints, quantum potentialities, and conscious participation.

1.5 Research Objectives

This work pursues four central aims:

1. **To articulate a multi-dimensional causational model of reality**, integrating physical, metaphysical, temporal, and quantum dimensions.
2. **To examine the causal role of consciousness** and its interaction with quantum processes.
3. **To explore the ontological status of the soul phenomenon,** evaluating whether it is a construct confined to this universe or a potentially transcendent entity.
4. **To synthesise scientific and philosophical perspectives** into a coherent ontology capable of addressing both structural and experiential aspects of existence.

1.6 Structure of the Book

The argument unfolds across three major parts:

- **Part I — The Scientific Model:** Introduces the multi-dimensional causational framework and its physical, metaphysical, temporal, and quantum components.

- **Part II — Consciousness and the Soul:** Examines consciousness as an emergent and participatory phenomenon and develops the concept of the soul as a quantum-informational substrate.
- **Part III — Synthesis and Implications:** Integrates the model into broader ontological and epistemological contexts, exploring its implications for identity, agency, and the participatory nature of reality.

1.7 Significance

By integrating insights from physics, metaphysics, information theory, consciousness studies, and ontology, this book contributes to a growing interdisciplinary effort to rethink the nature of reality. The model presented here challenges reductionist paradigms and reframes reality as both **structural** and **participatory**—a dynamic interplay between the universe's foundational dimensions and the conscious agents who inhabit it.

Ultimately, the work argues that **human agency is not incidental but central**: reality becomes meaningful and actualised through participation. This insight culminates in a reflection on the **participatory cosmos**, where consciousness and the soul phenomenon serve as the existential axis through which reality is co-created.

CHAPTER 2

FOUNDATIONS OF REALITY

2.1 Introduction

Any attempt to understand reality must confront the intertwined legacies of philosophy and science. Classical physics once offered a universe governed by strict determinism, a cosmos whose future could be predicted with absolute precision given sufficient information. The advent of quantum mechanics destabilised that vision, introducing uncertainty, probability, and the unsettling implication that observation may play a constitutive role in physical events. Meanwhile, cosmology situates existence within a dynamic, expanding universe shaped by entropy and deep temporal asymmetries.

This chapter surveys these foundational perspectives—classical, quantum, thermodynamic, and cosmological—not as isolated theories, but as complementary and sometimes competing attempts to describe what reality is. Their insights and limitations form the conceptual bedrock upon which the multi-dimensional causational model proposed in this book is built.

2.2 Classical Perspective: Reality as Objective Structure

For centuries, the prevailing scientific world-view treated reality as an objective, external structure governed by immutable laws. **Newtonian mechanics** famously captured this perspective, depicting the universe as a vast, clockwork system in which every event is the fully determined consequence of prior conditions.[1] This framework reinforced **scientific realism**, the view that physical entities exist independently of observation and that the task of science is to reveal the underlying structure of this objective world.[2]

Under this classical paradigm:

- **Matter and energy** form the fundamental constituents of reality.
- **Space and time** provide absolute, unchanging frameworks.

[1] Newton, I. *Philosophiæ Naturalis Principia Mathematica*. 1687

[2] Psillos, S. *Scientific Realism: How Science Tracks Truth*. Routledge, 1999

- **Causation** operates linearly, predictably, and without ambiguity.

This vision offered extraordinary explanatory and predictive power. Yet it left little conceptual space for phenomena that resist reduction to mechanical processes—subjective experience, agency, and the participatory role of observation. Classical physics described a world that could, in principle, unfold without witnesses.

2.3 The Quantum Revolution: Indeterminacy and Participation

The emergence of **quantum mechanics** in the early 20th century radically challenged classical assumptions. At microscopic scales, reality no longer appears deterministic. Instead, it exhibits:

- **Wave-particle duality**
- **Superposition**
- **Entanglement**

These features reveal a world structured not by certainty but by **probability**.[1] The notorious **observer**

[1] Heisenberg, W. *Physics and Philosophy: The Revolution in Modern Science*. Harper, 1958

effect—in which measurement alters the state of a system—suggests that observation is not merely passive but may actively shape the outcome of physical processes.[1]

Physicist John Wheeler captured the philosophical magnitude of this shift in his notion of a **"participatory universe"**, proposing that reality unfolds through acts of observation.[2] This idea challenges the traditional separation between observer and observed, raising profound questions:

- Is reality a fixed structure or a dynamic interplay between potentiality and observation?
- Does consciousness play a causal role in the collapse of quantum states?
- Is the universe fundamentally informational, relational, or interactive in nature?

Quantum theory therefore marks a turning point: it introduces participation as a potential ontological feature, not merely a methodological inconvenience.

[1] Bohr, N. "Discussion with Einstein on Epistemological Problems in Atomic Physics." In *Albert Einstein: Philosopher-Scientist*, 1949

[2] Wheeler, J. A. "Law Without Law." In *Quantum Theory and Measurement*, Princeton University Press, 1983

2.4 Entropy and Temporality

While quantum mechanics reshapes our understanding of microphysical processes, thermodynamics reframes our relationship with time. The **second law of thermodynamics** states that entropy—the measure of disorder—tends to increase in closed systems.[1] This principle establishes the **arrow of time**, making temporality directional, irreversible, and inescapable.

Entropy governs not only physical processes but also imposes a causational horizon on all phenomena:

- **Low-entropy origin:** The universe began in a state of extraordinary order.[2]
- **Heat-death scenario:** It may end in thermodynamic equilibrium, devoid of usable energy.[3]

These constraints extend to quantum and cosmological scales. Entropy is not merely a physical principle; it is a structural feature of reality that shapes the emergence, progression, and eventual dissolution

[1] Clausius, R. "On the Mechanical Theory of Heat." *Annalen der Physik*, 1850

[2] Carroll, S. *From Eternity to Here: The Quest for the Ultimate Theory of Time*. Dutton, 2010

[3] Davies, P. *The Last Three Minutes*. Basic Books, 1994

of complex systems.[1] In this sense, **temporality is not passive backdrop but active determinant.**

2.5 Cosmological Context

Modern cosmology deepens this picture by situating reality within an expanding universe driven by dark energy, gravitational curvature, and quantum fluctuations.[2] The origin of the universe's extraordinarily low-entropy initial state remains a major scientific puzzle, prompting competing hypotheses such as:

- **Cyclic cosmology**, in which the universe undergoes repeated cycles of birth and collapse.[3]
- **Multiverse theories**, which posit a vast ensemble of universes with varying physical laws.[4]

These proposals expand the conceptual scope of "reality," challenging the assumption that our observable cosmos is the totality of existence. They also underscore the limits of reductionist models, suggesting that

[1] Penrose, R. *The Road to Reality*. Vintage, 2005

[2] Hawking, S. *A Brief History of Time*. Bantam Books, 1988

[3] Steinhardt, P., & Turok, N. "A Cyclic Model of the Universe." *Science*, 2002

[4] Tegmark, M. *Our Mathematical Universe*. Knopf, 2014

current scientific paradigms may describe only a local manifestation of deeper structures.

2.6 Limitations of Current Paradigms

Despite their immense explanatory power, contemporary scientific models face persistent limitations:

- They cannot fully account for **subjective experience** or **conscious agency**.
- They struggle to explain the **participatory features** implied by quantum measurement.
- They offer no definitive account of the **origin of low entropy** or the **future of consciousness** in a thermodynamic universe.

These gaps signal the need for a broader ontology—one that integrates the physical, metaphysical, temporal, and quantum dimensions of existence with **the experiential and participatory aspects of being**.

The multi-dimensional causational model developed in the following chapters aims to provide such an integrative framework, reconciling structural explanations with the vital roles of meaning, observation, and consciousness.

PART II

-

THE MULTI-DIMENSIONAL CAUSATIONAL MODEL

CHAPTER 3

THE MULTI-DIMENSIONAL MODEL

3.1 Introduction

The preceding chapters exposed a persistent gap: while physics offers robust accounts of structure and causation, it does not capture subjective experience or the participatory character of knowing. This chapter develops the **Multi-Dimensional Causational Model**, which integrates **physical**, **metaphysical**, and **temporal** dimensions, underpinned by a quantum substrate and mediated by a **reality interface layer**. The model aims to show how structure and participation are not rivals but complements within a single ontological field.

In addition to joining these dimensions, the model treats **meaning** and **metaphysical coherence** as causal variables that shape the probability landscape of future states. Civilizations are not merely pushed by material constraints; they are **steered** by shared narratives, identity structures, and institutional architectures. These metaphysical forces widen or narrow the range of viable futures, rendering meaning itself a structural factor in the dynamics of reality.

3.2 Conceptual Foundations

The model is built on three primary dimensions:

- **Physical Reality** — the material substrate of existence.
- **Metaphysical Reality** — the domain of shared constructs and meaning.
- **Temporal Reality** — the irreversible progression of time shaped by entropy.

These dimensions interact within the **Reality Matrix of Causation**. Beneath this matrix lies the **Quantum Substrate**, a probabilistic informational layer enabling coherence and entanglement; above it sits the **Reality Interface Layer**, where observation and interpretation actualise potentiality into actuality. The following sections sketch each layer and its role in the wider ontology.

3.3 Dimension One: Physical Reality

Physical reality comprises matter, energy, and space—the observable constituents of the universe. Governed by physical laws, it provides the structural foundation for all phenomena; its regularities support both deterministic and probabilistic descriptions. The classical articulation of this vision—**laws, initial conditions, and predictability**—was given its canonical form in **Newtonian mechanics**, which pictured the cosmos as a lawful order whose dynamics unfold from precise principles and mathematically expressible forces.[1] Yet as powerful as this framework is, it does not, by itself, explain emergent properties like consciousness or the normativity of meaning.

3.4 Dimension Two: Metaphysical Reality

Metaphysical reality encompasses the social, cultural, and symbolic architectures through which we interpret the world and ourselves. It includes **language**, **ethics**, **ritual**, and **institutions**—features that exert causal influence even though they are not material in the narrow sense. A phenomenological point of departure helps: to exist is to be **already situated** in a meaningful world, practically oriented and interpretively engaged, rather than a detached spectator confronting bare data; this is the thrust of Heidegger's account of being-in-the-world.[2] On a sociological register, reality is **socially constructed** through the sedimentation of

[1] Newton, I. *Philosophiæ Naturalis Principia Mathematica.* 1687

[2] Heidegger, M. *Being and Time.* Harper & Row, 1962

meanings and institutionalization of roles, a process captured by Berger and Luckmann.[1]

Identity formation, moral orientation, and the very **sources of the self** are likewise historically layered and dialogical, as Taylor argues, which means that persons are formed within webs of significance rather than merely expressing internal preferences.[2] Such webs stabilise or destabilise moral practices, and this **moral architecture** influences collective resilience—an insight central to MacIntyre's analysis of traditions and the conditions for rational moral discourse.[3]

Beyond interpretation, metaphysical structures **do work.** They coordinate behaviour, stabilise expectations, and modulate risk. The social construction of reality is not merely descriptive; it is **causational**-shaping the range of achievable futures by enabling or impeding cooperation, trust, and institutional coherence.[4]

[1] Berger, P., & Luckmann, T. *The Social Construction of Reality*. Anchor Books, 1966

[2] Taylor, Charles. *Sources of the Self: The Making of the Modern Identity*. Harvard University Press, 1989

[3] MacIntyre, Alasdair. *After Virtue*. University of Notre Dame Press, 1981

[4] Berger, P., & Luckmann, T. *The Social Construction of Reality*. Anchor Books, 1966

3.5 Dimension Three: Temporal Reality

Temporal reality introduces irreversibility and progression. The **second law of thermodynamics** states that entropy—the measure of disorder—tends to increase in closed systems, thereby establishing the **arrow of time** and making temporality directional and inescapable.[1] Reichenbach formalised this asymmetry as a constitutive feature of causal ordering: the temporal orientation of cause to effect is not an artefact of description but a structural condition of experience and explanation.[2]

At cosmological scales, the **geometry of the universe** and the behaviour of gravitational degrees of freedom bear directly on entropy and the emergence of structure, a theme Penrose develops in his analysis of low-entropy boundary conditions and the deep puzzles of initial order.[3] In this sense, temporality is not a passive backdrop but an **active determinant** imposing horizons, constraints, and end-states on physical and metaphysical processes alike.

[1] Clausius, R. "On the Mechanical Theory of Heat." *Annalen der Physik*, 1850

[2] Reichenbach, H. *The Direction of Time*. University of California Press, 1956

[3] Penrose, R. *The Road to Reality*. Vintage, 2005

3.6 The Quantum Substrate

Beneath the matrix of physical, metaphysical, and temporal dimensions is the **quantum substrate**—a probabilistic informational field characterised by coherence, superposition, and entanglement. Philosophically, quantum theory disrupts the older ideal of detached observation: **measurement** is not merely registering what is but is bound up with the manifestation of outcomes; as Heisenberg stressed, the conditions of knowledge and the structure of the world are not neatly separable.[1]

Some proposals go further, suggesting that **conscious processes** may exploit quantum-level phenomena. The **Orch-OR** hypothesis, for instance, argues that quantum computations within neuronal microtubules could be relevant to consciousness, thereby linking neural dynamics to non-classical informational structures.[2] Independent of such speculative mechanisms, **quantum information theory** recasts coherence and entanglement as operational resources; in this framing,

[1] Heisenberg, W. *Physics and Philosophy: The Revolution in Modern Science.* Harper, 1958

[2] Hameroff, S., & Penrose, R. "Consciousness in the Universe: A Review of the Orch-OR Theory." *Physics of Life Reviews*, 2014

information is not a mere bookkeeping device but a primitive of physical theory.[1]

The interdependence of these layers becomes most visible when **metaphysical structures weaken**. When shared meaning dissolves, identity fragments, and truth becomes negotiable, institutions lose coherence. Classic analyses of political order indicate how **civilizational form** depends upon metaphysical orientation; the erosion of that orientation correlates with systemic fragility.[2] At the psychological-cultural level, the turn toward **expressive individualism** without shared norms can accelerate narcissistic dynamics that undermine solidarity and trust.[3] The result is a narrowed probability cone of viable futures and heightened susceptibility to technocratic or authoritarian substitutes for meaning.

3.7 Reality Interface Layer

Reality is neither wholly objective nor wholly subjective; it is an **interface layer** where world and mind meet. Observation **actualises** potentiality into determinate outcomes; experience is not a passive camera

[1] Michael A. Nielsen & Isaac L. Chuang. *Quantum Computation and Quantum Information*. Cambridge University Press, 2010

[2] Voegelin, Eric. *The New Science of Politics*. 1952

[3] Lasch, Christopher. *The Culture of Narcissism*. W. W. Norton, 1979

but an active participant. This motivates the model's **participatory** dimension: **consciousness** is not merely an epiphenomenon of neural activity but an agentive interface that organises information into coherent experience and influences the selection among possible futures.[1] In this register, consciousness is not a passive observer but an **ongoing participatory measurement process**. Each act of agency crosses the interface to actualise potentiality, and each outcome returns as experience through that same interface, requiring reinterpretation and reintegration before further action can occur.

3.8 Conceptual Multi-Dimensional Causational Model Diagram

Diagram 1 depicts the model's architecture: the Physical, Metaphysical, and Temporal dimensions rest upon the Quantum Substrate, while the Reality Interface Layer mediates the passage from potentiality to actuality. The diagram is heuristic; its purpose is to clarify roles and relations rather than to supply a single reductionist picture.

[1] Chalmers, D. *The Conscious Mind: In Search of a Fundamental Theory*. Oxford University Press, 1996

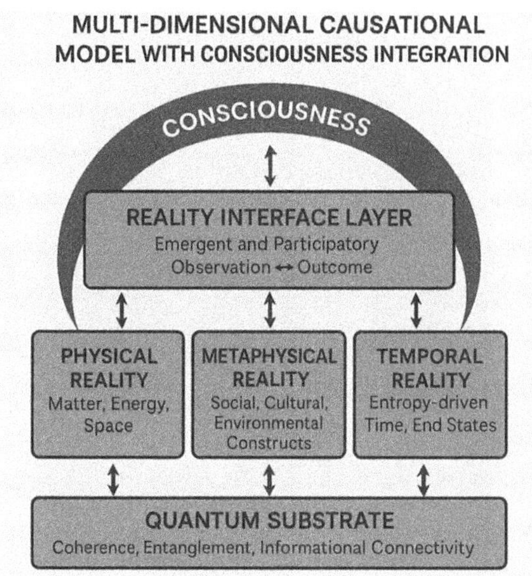

Diagram 1 - Multi-Dimensional Causational Model Concept

3.9 Growth and Endurance of the Soul Phenomenon

Figure 2 visualises a **single life-cone**. Originating at a luminous node (physical conception), the cone widens rapidly (growth and maximal potential) before tapering along the entropic time axis. A vertical plane marks the **present**, locally instantiating the model of Diagram 1. A faint continuation beyond the cone's tip gestures to the **possible endurance** of the soul phenomenon beyond physical death. Along this trajectory, the agent repeatedly crosses the reality interface: action actualises potential, consequence returns as experience, and identity is recursively revised rather than progressing in a single linear direction. The image is not empirical evidence but a conceptual aid to think **continuity**, **agency**, and **trajectory**.

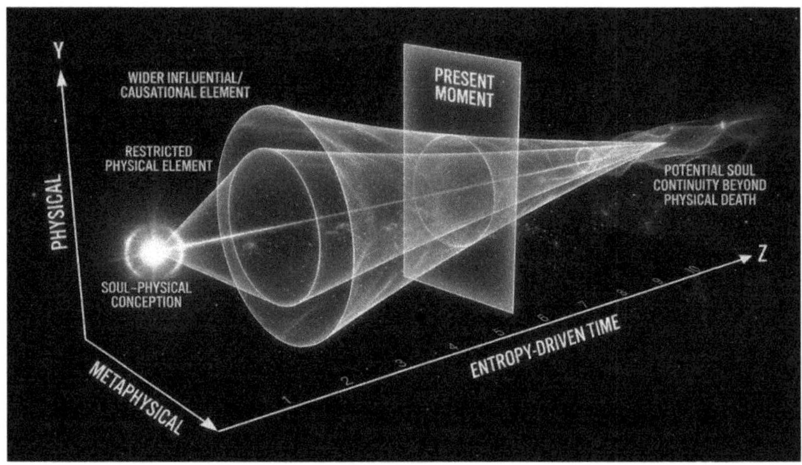

Figure 2 - Growth and Endurance of the Soul Phenomenon

3.10 Multiple Life Cones Across Entropic Time

Figure 3 extends the cone-grid to a **block-time** perspective, with multiple life-cones embedded within shared metaphysical, physical, and entropic coordinates. Overlapping cones highlight **collective influence** and **co-creation**: a single cone models individual agency; a cluster shows how interacting agents can reshape the metaphysical environment. Each cone represents not a fixed path but a series of recursive interface crossings, where collective and individual actions generate consequences that return as shared experience, reshaping future possibilities. The vertical plane labelled **"Present Moment"** intersects all cones, underscoring that actuality is always realised **together**, across persons and time.

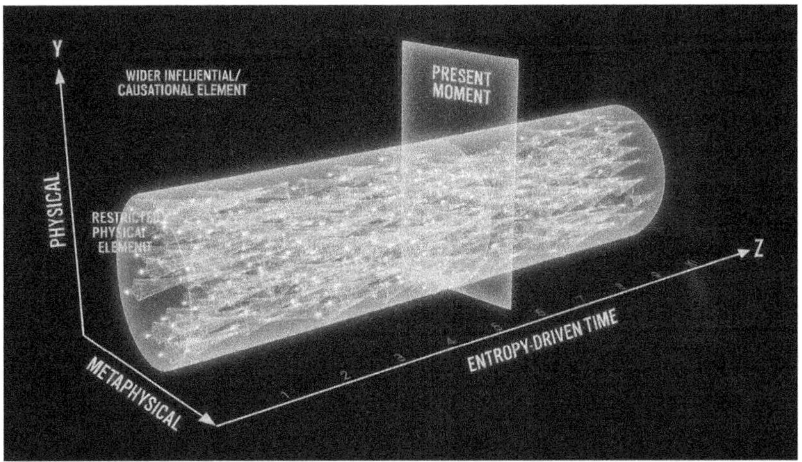

Figure 3 - Potential Influence of Multiple Life Cones on Reality

3.11 Identified Gap

The structural account remains incomplete without an account of **subjective experience** and **agency**. The gap motivates the introduction of **consciousness—and by extension, the soul phenomenon**—as the missing link that binds informational structure to lived actuality. Part III develops the claim of the gap, a missing participatory dimension, by introducing consciousness as the agent that activates potentiality.

3.12 Mathematical Representation of the Model

The mathematical expressions introduced here are heuristic and conceptual in intent. They are not meant to imply that metaphysical or conscious structures literally instantiate physical Hilbert spaces or formal quantum dynamics, but rather to provide a disciplined symbolic language for expressing relational structure, recursion, and probabilistic constraint.

The model can be expressed symbolically to foreground its logical structure. Let the primary dimensions **be Physical (P), Metaphysical (M), Temporal (T), and Quantum (Q); let Consciousness/Soul (C)** denote the participatory agent. Then the reality experienced at time t is:

$$R(t)=f(P(t),M(t),T(t),Q(t),C(t))$$

Because participation is recursive, the model also requires feedback updates:

$$C(t+1) = g(C(t),R(t))$$
$$M(t+1) = \mathrm{h}(M(t),R(t))$$

where realised reality feeds back into consciousness

and meaning, revising identity and re-weighting future agency.

subject to:

$$\frac{dS}{dt} \geq 0 \textit{ (entropy constraint)},$$

This entropy condition applies at the level of closed systems or the universe as a whole; local subsystems—organisms, institutions, or civilizations—may temporarily decrease entropy by exporting it. The constraint therefore encodes the global arrow of time without implying local monotonicity.

$$|\psi\rangle \rightarrow |\psi\_{i}\rangle \textit{ (state actualisation)}$$

This formulation is **heuristic** rather than empirical. It encodes that reality, as experienced, emerges from the interplay of structural dimensions **activated** by consciousness. The entropy condition encodes the **arrow of time**, a structural asymmetry central to causal explanation.[1] The quantum notation indicates the passage from **coherent potentiality** to **definite outcomes**.

[1] Reichenbach, H. *The Direction of Time*. University of California Press, 1956

3.13 Causational Ripples and Probabilistic Futures

Events—physical or metaphysical—do not terminate at the moment of occurrence; they **propagate** along the model's axes, reshaping the probability distribution of future states. The ripples accumulate, biasing potential outcomes prior to collapse into actuality. In cognitive domains, empirical work suggests that decision-making can exhibit **quantum-probabilistic** signatures—contextuality, order effects, and interference—rather than strictly classical aggregation.[1] This line of research has developed into formal **quantum models of cognition and decision**, capturing how meaning and context modulate choice in ways that mirror quantum structure.[2] These ripples are not merely external effects: they return to the agent as experienced consequences, shaping interpretation, meaning, and the next cycle of participation.

Within the model, **probability cones** track how futures widen or narrow. **Physical entropy** tends to narrow cones over time; **metaphysical coherence** can widen or stabilise them by lowering coordination costs

[1] Jerome R. Busemeyer & Zheng Wang, "Quantum Cognition: Modeling Behavior in Entangled Contexts," *Current Directions in Psychological Science* 24, no. 6 (2015): 442–448

[2] Busemeyer, J. R., & Bruza, P. D. *Quantum Models of Cognition and Decision*. Cambridge University Press, 2012

and increasing shared expectation. The **causal graph** of a system—how variables influence one another—can be explicitly shaped by interventions, policies, or commitments; a mature theory of **causal inference** clarifies how such interventions alter the distribution of outcomes.[1]

3.14 Mathematical Notes on Causational Ripples

Formally, the ripple effect can be expressed as a state update across the model's axes. Let the joint state be ρ_t over the Hilbert spaces of Physical H_P, Metaphysical H_M, and Quantum H_Q, evolving along the Temporal axis (T).

Joint state: $\rho_t \in H_P \otimes H_M \otimes H_Q$

Here the Hilbert spaces H_P, H_M, and H_Q function as abstract informational state spaces rather than literal quantum fields. This notation provides a formal idiom for contextuality, updating, and probabilistic reweighting without implying that metaphysical structures possess quantum physical properties.

An event functions as an intervention operator E, updating the state: $\rho_{t+1} = E(\rho_t)$

Future probabilities can be written as: $P(\text{future state} \mid \rho_{t+1}) = \mathrm{Tr}(\Pi \rho_{t+1})$

[1] Pearl, J. *Causality: Models, Reasoning, and Inference.* Cambridge University Press, 2009

This schematic aligns with efforts to formulate quantum theory in **inference-theoretic** terms that are neutral with respect to causal direction,[1] while remaining compatible with **interventionist** treatments of causality in complex systems.[2] Together they provide a formal idiom for articulating how **choices** and **events** reweight the cone of probabilistic futures.

3.15 Synthesis

The **Multi-Dimensional Causational Model** depicts reality as a field where **structure** and **participation** co-determine what becomes actual. Physical, temporal, and quantum constraints set the boundaries of possibility; **metaphysical coherence**—sustained by narratives, identities, and institutions—governs whether civilizations **flourish** or **fragment**. In the chapters that follow, we turn to the **participatory agent** itself—consciousness and the soul—to complete the ontology of a world that is at once **given** and **co-created**.

[1] Leifer, M. S., & Spekkens, R. W. "Towards a formulation of quantum theory as a causally neutral theory of Bayesian inference." *Physical Review A*, 88(5), 2013

[2] Pearl, J. *Causality: Models, Reasoning, and Inference*. Cambridge University Press, 2009

PART III

-

CONSCIOUSNESS, THE SOUL, AND PARTICIPATORY REALITY

CHAPTER 4

CONSCIOUSNESS AS EMERGENT AND PARTICIPATORY

4.1 Introduction

Having established cone-grid visualisations of individual growth and collective block-time interaction, we now turn to **consciousness**—not merely as a late emergent of neural complexity, but as a **participatory agent** that activates trajectories and co-creates actuality within the quantum substrate. Despite striking advances in cognitive science, consciousness remains a central enigma: empirical models describe mechanisms for attention, memory, and perception, yet they do not resolve the **hard problem**—why and how subjective experience exists at all.[1] In the account developed here, consciousness is **emergent and participatory**: it arises from organised material and informational processes while also

[1] Chalmers, D. *The Conscious Mind: In Search of a Fundamental Theory.* Oxford University Press, 1996

playing a constitutive role in actualising potential states of reality.

To understand consciousness as participatory is also to recognise the uniquely human capacity for **metaphysical navigation**—the aptitude to construct, inhabit, and act within symbolic worlds that exceed immediate stimuli and reshape the field of possible futures.

4.2 Classical and Neuroscientific Views

Classical and contemporary neuroscience broadly construes consciousness as an **emergent property** of complex neural networks. On this view, coherent mental life arises from electrochemical signalling and large-scale neuronal integration, yielding the familiar capacities of perception, memory, and attention.[1] Yet three puzzles persist:

- **Qualia**: the irreducible "what-it-is-like" quality of experience, which eludes purely functional description.[2]
- **Unity**: the integration of distributed neural events into a single, first-person perspective.

[1] Edelman, G. *Bright Air, Brilliant Fire: On the Matter of the Mind*. Basic Books, 1992

[2] Chalmers, D. *The Conscious Mind: In Search of a Fundamental Theory*. Oxford University Press, 1996

- **Agency**: the apparent efficacy of intention in guiding outcomes rather than merely reporting them.

These lacunae motivate exploration beyond strict classical frameworks—without abandoning scientific discipline—to consider whether non-classical processes might be implicated in how experience becomes unified and causally efficacious.

4.3 Quantum Consciousness Theories

A family of proposals investigates whether **quantum phenomena** are relevant to consciousness:

- **Von Neumann–Wigner interpretation**: the suggestion that conscious observation plays a role in **wavefunction collapse**, implicating mind in the selection of outcomes rather than treating measurement as wholly external to experience.[1]
- **Orchestrated objective reduction (Orch-OR)**: the hypothesis that quantum computations within **neuronal microtubules** contribute to consciousness, linking cognitive events to non-classical

[1] Wigner, E. P. "Remarks on the Mind-Body Question." In *Symmetries and Reflections*. Indiana University Press, 1967

informational structures and objective reduction processes.[1]

- **Participatory universe (Wheeler)**: the idea that acts of observation are constitutive in the emergence of reality; the universe "becomes" through participatory measurement rather than pre-existing as a fully determinate backdrop.[2]

Philosophically, these positions resonate with a broader insight from quantum foundations: the conditions of knowledge and the structure of the world are not cleanly separable—**measurement** is entangled with manifestation.[3] Empirical adjudication remains ongoing and contested, but such theories provide **bridging concepts** between physical description and lived experience by treating information, observation, and actuality as mutually implicating.

4.4 Consciousness as a Participatory Agent

If consciousness can couple—even subtly—to quantum-informational states, reality is not a fixed

[1] Hameroff, S., & Penrose, R. "Consciousness in the Universe: A Review of the Orch-OR Theory." *Physics of Life Reviews*, 2014

[2] Wheeler, J. A. "Law Without Law." In *Quantum Theory and Measurement*. Princeton University Press, 1983

[3] Heisenberg, W. *Physics and Philosophy: The Revolution in Modern Science*. Harper, 1958

tableau but a **participatory continuum**. Observation does not merely reveal pre-existing facts; it **actualises** potentialities into definite outcomes, situating the observer at the interface where information becomes physically determinate—an interface that, at the level of lived reality, is registered as experience.[1 2] In this register, consciousness is both **emergent** (arising from organised complexity) and **causal** (biasing probabilistic pathways within lawful constraints). This stance coheres with Wheeler's participatory universe and with Orch-OR's suggestion that **non-classical** informational substrates may matter to experience.[3 4]

Human Cognition as Metaphysical Navigation. Human beings do not only perceive; we **interpret**, **narrate**, and **project** meaning. Our engagements are mediated by symbolic forms—language, norms, ritual, and culture—that structure cognition and action beyond immediate stimuli. Scheler emphasises the distinctive depth of the person and the hierarchy of values disclosed through intentional life, setting

[1] Heisenberg, W. *Physics and Philosophy: The Revolution in Modern Science*. Harper, 1958

[2] Wheeler, J. A. "Law Without Law." In *Quantum Theory and Measurement*. Princeton University Press, 1983

[3] Wheeler, J. A. "Law Without Law." In *Quantum Theory and Measurement*. Princeton University Press, 1983

[4] Hameroff, S., & Penrose, R. "Consciousness in the Universe: A Review of the Orch-OR Theory." *Physics of Life Reviews*, 2014

human subjectivity apart by its openness to the world of spirit (Geist).[1] Cassirer, in turn, portrays the human as *animal symbolicum*, constituted by the symbolic forms that organise knowledge and culture.[2] Read together, these insights suggest that consciousness is not a mere adaptive computation but a **participatory interface** with deeper dimensions of reality—one through which meaning becomes a causal factor shaping the space of possible futures. This deepening of interiority echoes Teilhard de Chardin's proposal that the cosmos exhibits a directional tendency toward **increasing complexity and self-awareness**, with consciousness both signalling and driving the unfolding of reality.[3]

This participatory capacity presupposes an underlying informational continuity—a topic examined in Chapter 5 under the concept of the soul phenomenon

4.5 Implications for Reality

As argued in Chapter 3, metaphysical coherence forms part of the causal landscape; consciousness

[1] Scheler, Max. *The Human Place in the Cosmos.* Northwestern University Press, 2009

[2] Cassirer, Ernst. *An Essay on Man.* Yale University Press, 1944

[3] Pierre Teilhard de Chardin. *The Phenomenon of Man.* Harper & Brothers, 1955

influences this landscape from the inside. The participatory character of consciousness challenges **reductionist** paradigms on several fronts:

- **Ontological status**: Reality is not wholly objective; it is **co-created** in acts of observation and interpretation.[1][2]
- **Agency**: Consciousness introduces **intentional causation** within probabilistic constraints, influencing which of many viable futures becomes actual.[3][4]
- **Relationality**: The universe may be fundamentally **informational and relational**, with consciousness as a constitutive component rather than a dispensable epiphenomenon.[5][6]

[1] Wheeler, J. A. "Law Without Law." In *Quantum Theory and Measurement*. Princeton University Press, 1983

[2] Heisenberg, W. *Physics and Philosophy: The Revolution in Modern Science*. Harper, 1958

[3] Hameroff, S., & Penrose, R. "Consciousness in the Universe: A Review of the Orch-OR Theory." *Physics of Life Reviews*, 2014

[4] Wigner, E. P. "Remarks on the Mind-Body Question." In *Symmetries and Reflections*. Indiana University Press, 1967

[5] Wheeler, J. A. "Law Without Law." In *Quantum Theory and Measurement*. Princeton University Press, 1983

[6] Heisenberg, W. *Physics and Philosophy: The Revolution in Modern Science*. Harper, 1958

Yet consciousness alone does not explain the **unity**, **continuity**, and **moral orientation** of the participatory agent. These call for a more enduring interior principle—here named the **soul phenomenon**—which the next chapter examines in detail as the substrate that sustains identity, agency, and meaning across time. In Chapter 6, we return to participation at scale, analysing how agency aligns with or undermines **metaphysical coherence** in civilisational fields.

CHAPTER 5

THE SOUL PHENOMENON

5.1 Introduction

The preceding chapter positioned consciousness as an emergent yet **participatory agent** within the multi-dimensional causational model, suggesting that meaning exerts causal force and that observation participates in the collapse of potentiality. If those claims hold, there must be an enduring interior structure that anchors unity, continuity, and agency across time—here named the **soul phenomenon**. This chapter asks two linked questions: *What is the soul phenomenon, and how does it relate to consciousness and reality?* Is the soul best conceived as **intra-cosmic**—a quantum-informational substrate within this universe—or as **transcendent**, persisting across or beyond cosmological horizons? The discussion integrates scientific proposals with philosophical reasoning, acknowledging empirical limits while exploring **plausible ontological trajectories**.

5.2 Defining the Soul Beyond Religious Constructs

Across intellectual history, the **soul** has often been treated as a metaphysical principle of life and agency, a topic central to classical philosophy and subsequently to theological traditions.[1] In this monograph, however, the soul is framed not doctrinally but **ontologically**: a **quantum-informational substrate** that sustains coherence, identity, and agency over time. On this view, **consciousness** is the active expression of that substrate—its participatory interface with the world—through which potentiality is collapsed into meaningful actuality. This interiority is not sealed within the psyche: the soul remains continuously coupled to the reality interface, integrating experience across repeated participatory crossings rather than containing identity as a closed system.

The Soul as Informational Substrate

Within the multi-dimensional model, the soul functions as a **coherence-preserving field**: a probabilistic, entanglement-capable substrate that mediates between quantum potentiality and lived experience, enabling unified awareness, persistent identity, and efficacious

[1] Aristotle. *De Anima*. 350 BCE

agency.[1 2] Empirical precedents for biological quantum effects, while still developing, include indications of **coherence and entanglement** in living systems (e.g., photosynthesis, avian magnetoreception), suggesting that organisms can exploit quantum resources at non-trivial scales.[3] Moreover, anaesthetic studies on **microtubules**—key cytoskeletal components in neurons—show disruption patterns during loss of consciousness consistent with a role in **quantum-level informational processes.**[4] These findings do not prove a "soul" in any theological sense, but they **strengthen the conceptual plausibility** of an informational substrate that could underwrite conscious participation in reality.

5.3 Growth and Endurance of the Soul

The **cone-grid** visualisation (Chapter 3, Figure 2) captures how the soul's informational substrate relates

[1] Hameroff, S., & Penrose, R. "Consciousness in the Universe: A Review of the Orch OR Theory." *Physics of Life Reviews*, 2014

[2] Craddock, T. J. A., et al. "Anaesthetic Alterations of Microtubule Function Suggest a Role in Consciousness." *Frontiers in Psychology*, 2015

[3] Lambert, N., Chen, Y. N., Cheng, Y. C., Li, C. M., Chen, G. Y., & Nori, F. (2013). "Quantum Biology." *Nature Physics*, 9(1), 10–18

[4] Craddock, T. J. A., et al. (2015). "Anaesthetic alterations of microtubule function suggest a role in consciousness." *Frontiers in Psychology*, 6, 1–12

to human development and entropic decline, while leaving open the question of **endurance beyond death**. Neuroscientific timing studies show that **probabilistic neural activity** can precede reportable conscious intention by milliseconds, leaving room (conceptually) for a **preconscious interface** where indeterminate states are resolved into awareness and action.[1] If such preconscious dynamics involve quantum processes, this interface could be the locus where the soul's informational substrate **translates probabilistic structure into experienced agency**.

5.4 Option A: The Soul as a Quantum-Informational Field

One hypothesis situates the soul entirely **within this universe** as a non-corporeal quantum phenomenon:

- **Rooted in coherence and entanglement** at the level of the quantum substrate, making agency possible within probabilistic constraints.[2]
- **Functioning as an informational field** that enables consciousness to emerge and persist,

[1] Libet, B. (1985). "Unconscious cerebral initiative and the role of conscious will in voluntary action." *Behavioral and Brain Sciences*, 8(4), 529–566

[2] Heisenberg, W. *Physics and Philosophy: The Revolution in Modern Science*. Harper, 1958

consistent with proposals linking microtubular quantum processes to aspects of awareness.[1]
- **Subject to entropy and eventual decoherence**, implying a **finite end state** governed by thermodynamic and quantum principles.[2]

This view aligns with **Orch-OR** and with **participatory** interpretations of observation, locating the soul's efficacy **inside** the universe's lawful and informational horizons while declining to ascribe it independent metaphysical substance.[3 4]

Implication: If Option A is correct, the soul's persistence is **finite**: it can endure as long as coherence can be maintained but ultimately faces the boundary conditions of this cosmos.

5.5 Option B: The Soul as Transcendent

A second hypothesis treats the soul as **transcendent** relative to our cosmos, participating in a wider ontological cycle:

[1] Hameroff, S., & Penrose, R. "Consciousness in the Universe: A Review of the Orch OR Theory." *Physics of Life Reviews*, 2014

[2] Penrose, R. *The Road to Reality*. Vintage, 2005

[3] Hameroff, S., & Penrose, R. "Consciousness in the Universe: A Review of the Orch OR Theory." *Physics of Life Reviews*, 2014

[4] Hameroff, S., & Penrose, R. "Consciousness in the Universe: A Review of the Orch-OR Theory." *Physics of Life Reviews*, 2014

- **Cyclic cosmology:** the universe undergoes repeated expansions and contractions; informational structures could, in principle, have **non-local continuity** across cycles.[1]
- **Multiverse theories:** our universe may be one among many, with the possibility (speculative but not incoherent) of **informational persistence** across domains with distinct laws.[2]
- **Quantum vacuum fluctuations:** the vacuum can be modelled as a sea of **pre-spacetime potentialities**, gesturing toward informational substrates that are not constrained by classical spacetime boundaries.[3]

Implication: If Option B is correct, the soul's identity may be **rooted in a deeper ontological continuum**, with our universe as a local manifestation of a more comprehensive informational order.

5.6 Philosophical Extrapolation

Philosophically, the soul phenomenon strains reductionism and invites a **relational ontology**. If

[1] Steinhardt, P., & Turok, N. "A Cyclic Model of the Universe." *Science*, 2002

[2] Tegmark, M. *Our Mathematical Universe*. Knopf, 2014

[3] Davies, P. *The Last Three Minutes*. Basic Books, 1994

observation and meaning co-create actuality, then the soul can be interpreted as the **continuity of agency** that outlives any single physical configuration—whether that continuity is intra-cosmic (Option A) or trans-cosmic (Option B). This raises questions concerning identity, teleology, and value beyond physical dissolution. The theme resonates with cultural-symbolic accounts in which **shared meanings** constitute realities we inhabit and through which we act,[1] as well as with **temporal** analyses that anchor causation to the arrow of time while acknowledging horizons and end-states.[2] In this spirit, Teilhard de Chardin's vision of co-creation can be read as a theological analogue to a participatory ontology in which human agency collaborates with a larger cosmic order.

5.7 Limitations and Speculative Nature

- **No direct empirical evidence:** There is **no conclusive empirical proof** for the soul as either a quantum-informational field or a transcendent substrate; the arguments here are **conceptual and exploratory**.

[1] Berger, P., & Luckmann, T. *The Social Construction of Reality*. Anchor Books, 1966

[2] Reichenbach, H. *The Direction of Time*. University of California Press, 1956

- **Suggestive, not decisive:** Quantum-biological and microtubule studies are **suggestive** rather than definitive; interpretations remain contested.[1 2]
- **Methodological humility:** The use of quantum and cosmological frameworks is intended to **clarify possibilities**, not to overstep evidential bounds. The proposals complement, rather than replace, scientific inquiry.

In sum, this chapter has articulated two live hypotheses about the soul's ontological status while preserving **epistemic caution**. The model proceeds by treating the soul phenomenon as the enduring interior axis of agency and meaning—the **informational coherence** through which consciousness participates in reality, whether finitely **within** this universe or as part of a **larger** ontological horizon.

[1] Lambert, N., Chen, Y. N., Cheng, Y. C., Li, C. M., Chen, G. Y., & Nori, F. (2013). "Quantum Biology." *Nature Physics*, 9(1), 10–18

[2] Craddock, T. J. A., et al. (2015). "Anaesthetic alterations of microtubule function suggest a role in consciousness." *Frontiers in Psychology*, 6, 1–12

PART IV

-

MEANING, AGENCY, AND CIVILIZATIONAL FUTURES

CHAPTER 6

AGENCY, MEANING, AND CIVILIZATIONAL CAUSATION

6.1 Introduction

The preceding chapters developed a multidimensional causational ontology in which reality arises from the interplay of physical, metaphysical, temporal, and quantum-informational dimensions, activated by consciousness and sustained by the soul phenomenon. We now extend this framework into the **collective domain**. Civilizations are not merely historical aggregates or sociological abstractions; they are **metaphysical fields**—shared environments of meaning within which identity, behaviour, and agency take form.[1]

On this view, civilizational trajectories—flourishing, stagnation, fragmentation, or collapse—cannot be reduced to material forces alone. They reflect the **coherence or breakdown** of shared meanings, the **alignment**

[1] Berger, P., & Luckmann, T. *The Social Construction of Reality*. Anchor Books, 1966

or inversion of agency, and the **widening or narrowing** of the probability landscape of collective futures. What follows introduces *creation-aligned* and *negation-aligned* agency, the *civilizational field*, and *probability cones*, integrating them within the book's broader ontology and preparing the ground for the concluding synthesis.

6.2 The Civilizational Field as a Metaphysical Structure

Civilizations can be understood as fields of **shared meaning**—collective metaphysical environments that shape who we become and how we act together. These fields emerge from narratives and symbols, moral frameworks and institutions, and the memory that binds generations into a living tradition. As argued in Chapter 3, metaphysical structures exert causal force by shaping the **probability landscape** of future states; at scale, civilizations therefore possess **collective probability cones**, ranges of viable futures determined by the coherence of their shared architecture.[1 2]

When shared meaning is strong, identity is integrated, institutions are trusted, and coordination costs

[1] Berger, P., & Luckmann, T. *The Social Construction of Reality.* Anchor Books, 1966

[2] Reichenbach, H. *The Direction of Time.* University of California Press, 1956

are low. The civilizational probability cone **widens**, enabling innovation, resilience, and adaptive capacity. When meaning fragments—when truth becomes negotiable and identity unmoored—the cone **narrows**, viable trajectories diminish, and systems become fragile.

6.3 Agency as a Collective Causal Force

Earlier chapters treated agency as the soul's participatory capacity to collapse potentiality into actuality. That capacity **scales**, generating patterns of collective action. The aggregated agency of millions of persons—acting within a shared metaphysical field and integrating the consequences of prior action—produces **civilizational trajectories**. In causal terms, the civilizational field is a graph of interdependent variables in which interventions, commitments, and norms alter the distribution of outcomes; **agency** reorganizes the graph and **reweights** the futures it makes available.[1]

Crucially, agency is not neutral. It polarises along two orientations:

- **Creation-aligned agency**
- **Negation-aligned agency**

[1] Pearl, J. *Causality: Models, Reasoning, and Inference*. Cambridge University Press, 2009

These are not moral labels but **causational dynamics** that determine whether a civilization expands or contracts its probability cone.

6.4 Creation-Aligned Agency

Creation-aligned agency arises when persons and communities are anchored in coherent meanings and oriented toward the good. It is characterised by:

- **Coherence-building:** reinforcing shared meaning and institutional stability.
- **Future-expanding:** generating technological, moral, and cultural possibilities.
- **Responsibility-oriented:** recognising the causal weight of intention.
- **Meaning-affirming:** strengthening the metaphysical field.

In teleological terms, creation-aligned agency rides with the grain of an ordered cosmos, contributing to increasing complexity, interiority, and creative advance.[1] Where such agency predominates, the civilizational probability cone **widens**—not as a naïve optimism, but

[1] Pierre Teilhard de Chardin. *The Phenomenon of Man*. Harper & Brothers, 1955

as the structural consequence of integrated meaning and disciplined action.

6.5 Negation-Aligned Agency

Negation-aligned agency emerges when meaning collapses, identity fragments, or persons become unable—or feel unable—to participate in shaping their world. When the soul's participatory function is obstructed, agency **inverts**: instead of generating coherence, it reacts against it. Negation-aligned agency is marked by:

- **Coherence-dissolving:** fragmenting shared meaning and eroding trust.
- **Future-narrowing:** reducing the range of viable possibilities.
- **Ressentiment-driven:** acting from perceived powerlessness.
- **Meaning-destructive:** attacking the structures that enable common action.

This pattern is diagnostically visible in cultures of narcissism and performative rupture, where interior emptiness seeks public confirmation in ways that corrode solidarity.[1] As negation-aligned agency spreads,

[1] Lasch, Christopher. *The Culture of Narcissism*. W. W. Norton, 1979

the civilizational probability cone **contracts**, accelerating institutional decay and social fatigue.

6.6 Probability Cones and Civilizational Trajectories

Probability cones translate civilizational dynamics into a **probabilistic geometry**. The wider the cone, the more pathways remain open; the narrower the cone, the more a society is trapped by its own entropy. The **arrow of time**—the increasing entropy that structures temporality—establishes an irreducible asymmetry: left unattended, systems drift toward disorder, narrowing their future options.[1] Yet this drift is not fate. Through intentional interventions—policies, practices, and moral commitments—communities can **re-shape** their causal graphs, altering the probabilities of what becomes actual.[2] At large scales, physical constraints (including gravitational and thermodynamic structure) set outer bounds on what is possible, but within those bounds, **meaning and agency** modulate how futures unfold.[3]

[1] Reichenbach, H. *The Direction of Time*. University of California Press, 1956

[2] Pearl, J. *Causality: Models, Reasoning, and Inference*. Cambridge University Press, 2009

[3] Penrose, R. *The Road to Reality*. Vintage, 2005

- **Widening cones** correspond to periods of flourishing, innovation, and stability.
- **Narrowing cones** correspond to fragmentation, institutional decay, and heightened existential risk.

Seen in this light, civilizational history is not a sequence of accidents, but an ordered record of **coherence gained or lost**.

6.7 Meaning as a Civilizational Variable

Meaning is not merely interpretive; it is **causal**. Shared meaning:

- stabilises the civilizational field,
- integrates identity,
- enables coordination,
- sustains institutions, and
- anchors agency.

Where meaning collapses, people retreat into **micro-worlds** of private significance; institutions lose legitimacy; and collective purpose withers.[1] Conversely, when a society renews its sources of meaning—its

[1] Taylor, Charles. *Sources of the Self: The Making of the Modern Identity*. Harvard University Press, 1989

moral vision, symbolic grammar, and public goods—its probability cone widens. *What* a people holds to be true and good is not epiphenomenal to its survival; it is structural.

6.8 Civilizational Replacement Dynamics

Civilizations with weak metaphysical cores become vulnerable to **replacement** by systems with stronger coherence—religious, ideological, or technocratic. Replacement is not fundamentally demographic; it is **metaphysical**. A robust meaning-architecture exerts gravitational pull; a weak one dissipates. Put differently, **order** is not sustained by material force alone but by participation in a meaningful cosmos.[1] Replacement occurs when one system's probability cone **expands** (through renewed coherence and agency) while another's **collapses**.

6.9 The Role of Consciousness and the Soul in Collective Reality

The participatory model of consciousness developed in Chapters 4 and 5 extends naturally to the collective. If individual consciousness collapses potentiality into actuality, then **collective consciousness**

[1] Voegelin, Eric. *The New Science of Politics*. 1952

collapses collective potentialities into **shared actualities**—through rituals, laws, norms, and narratives that define *what is possible together.*[1] The **soul phenomenon**, as locus of agency and meaning, thus scales upward: from interior participation to civilizational causation. Civilizational trajectories are not merely historical patterns; they are expressions of **collective interiority**.

6.10 Summary

This chapter has integrated the ontology of reality with a civilizational framework grounded in **agency, meaning, and probabilistic causation**. We have shown that:

- civilizations are **metaphysical fields**;
- agency **scales** into collective forms;
- meaning functions as a **causal variable**;
- probability cones model **civilizational futures**;
- metaphysical coherence governs **resilience**; and
- the **soul phenomenon** underlies both individual and collective causation.

[1] Wheeler, J. A. "Law Without Law." In *Quantum Theory and Measurement*. Princeton University Press, 1983

Read in concert with Chapters 4 and 5, these claims prepare the ground for the concluding synthesis: an account of reality as an interface where structure and participation co-determine what becomes actual.

PART V

-

SYNTHESIS AND IMPLICATIONS

CHAPTER 7

WHAT IS REALITY? (EPISTEMOLOGICAL SYNTHESIS)

7.1 Introduction

The preceding chapters developed a multi-dimensional causational model in which reality arises from the interplay of physical, metaphysical, temporal, and quantum-informational dimensions, activated by consciousness and sustained by the soul phenomenon. We now turn to the central question itself: **What is reality?** Is it an objective structure, a participatory continuum, or a relational construct? Answering requires an **epistemological synthesis** that draws together physical theory, quantum foundations, and phenomenological accounts of meaning.

7.2 Physicalist Interpretation: Reality as Objective Structure

From a **physicalist** standpoint, reality is the totality of entities and processes governed by lawful regularities. On this view:

- **Independence:** Reality exists regardless of observation.
- **Determinism (or at least law-governed evolution):** Events unfold according to lawful causal chains.
- **Empiricism:** Knowledge derives from observation and measurement.

Scientific realism refines this picture by claiming that well-confirmed theories approximate truth about a mind-independent world.[1] This interpretation underwrites the extraordinary success of modern science. Yet, taken alone, it struggles to account for **subjective experience** and for those **measurement-dependent** features of quantum theory that appear to entangle observation with outcome.

[1] Psillos, S. *Scientific Realism: How Science Tracks Truth*. Routledge, 1999

7.3 Participatory Interpretation: Reality as Co-Created

Quantum mechanics disrupts the ideal of a wholly detached observer. Phenomena associated with measurement—contextuality, indeterminacy, and the collapse problem—have led some to propose that **observation participates** in bringing about definite outcomes. **Wheeler's** notion of a *participatory universe* highlights this entanglement: acts of measurement help determine "what happens," not merely record it.[1] In a complementary philosophical register, the analysis of **measurement** emphasises that the conditions of knowledge and the structure of the world are not cleanly separable.[2]

If consciousness interacts with quantum states, reality looks:

- **Probabilistic:** actuality emerging from potentiality,
- **Dynamic:** observation functioning as a causal agent,

[1] Wheeler, J. A. "Law Without Law." In *Quantum Theory and Measurement*. Princeton University Press, 1983

[2] Heisenberg, W. *Physics and Philosophy: The Revolution in Modern Science*. Harper, 1958

- **Relational:** outcomes contingent on informational exchange and experimental context.[1]

This interpretive arc elevates **agency** from observer to participant, suggesting that reality is, at least in part, **co-created** through observation and interpretation.

7.4 Epistemological Interpretation: Reality as Relational Construct

Phenomenology and relational ontology argue that reality is **disclosed** through interpretation within shared worlds of meaning. **Heidegger**'s account of being-in-the-world situates knowing as an engaged, practical comportment rather than a view from nowhere.[2] In social theory, **Berger & Luckmann** show how institutions, language, and norms sediment into a *social construction of reality*, through which communities stabilise expectations and coordinate action.[3] In this light:

- **Contextuality:** Reality is mediated by language, culture, practice.

[1] Heisenberg, W. *Physics and Philosophy: The Revolution in Modern Science.* Harper, 1958

[2] Heidegger, M. *Being and Time.* Harper & Row, 1962

[3] Berger, P., & Luckmann, T. *The Social Construction of Reality.* Anchor Books, 1966

- **Intersubjectivity:** Knowledge is co-constructed within shared frameworks.
- **Limits:** Access to the real is filtered by perceptual and conceptual horizons.

This perspective does not deny a world independent of us; it claims that our *access* to that world is constitutively interpretive.

7.5 Integrative Model: Reality as Interface

Synthesised, these interpretations yield a picture of reality as an **interface** where structural and experiential dimensions meet:

- **Ontological Basis:** Physical, metaphysical, and temporal dimensions provide the **structure** of possibility (from classical lawfulness to entropic constraints).
- **Informational Substrate:** Quantum coherence and entanglement provide a field of **probabilistic potential**.
- **Experiential Activation: Consciousness** actualises potentiality into **experienced actuality**.
- **Participatory Mediation:** The **soul phenomenon** sustains informational **continuity** of agency and meaning across time.

This integrative stance coheres with the symbolic formulation of §3.12, where the real at time *t* is modelled as a function of structural dimensions **activated** by consciousness. In this register, the cone-grid visualisations (Chapter 3) are **heuristic**: not empirical diagrams but conceptual aids for grasping how physical structure, temporal asymmetry, and participatory agency interlock.

Wheeler's "It from Bit" captures the same intuition from another angle: at bottom, the world may be **informational**, with bits of information—registered through acts of distinction and measurement—playing a constitutive role in what becomes actual.[1] Within this framework, the soul phenomenon can be construed as an **informational substrate** that maintains coherence and identity, enabling consciousness to transform potential into actuality without implying reduction to matter alone.

Thus, reality is neither purely objective nor merely subjective; it is a **participatory continuum**—emergent, dynamic, and relational. Consciousness and the soul are not peripheral anomalies but central **agents of co-creation** within the multi-dimensional causational model.

[1] Wheeler, J. A. "Information, Physics, Quantum: The Search for Links." In *Complexity, Entropy, and the Physics of Information.* Addison-Wesley, 1990

7.6 Identity and Agency Across Individual and Population Levels

The integrative model bears directly on **identity** and **agency**. At the **individual** level, identity can be understood as the continuity of **informational patterns** across time, sustained by the soul phenomenon; each act of choice produces **ripples** that update both self-concept and trajectory of agency. At the individual level, identity is best understood as a recursive continuity of informational patterns, continuously revised as action crosses the reality interface and returns as consequence requiring reinterpretation. Agency, therefore, is not a static possession but a **participatory function** embedded in probabilistic futures.[1]

At the **population** level, overlapping cones (Figure 3) illustrate how **collective agency** emerges from interactions among individual ripples. Shared metaphysical constructs—language, ethics, culture—mediate these interactions and distribute causal power across institutions and practices.[2] Meanwhile, decision-making research shows that human choices can exhibit **quantum-probabilistic** signatures (context effects,

[1] Archer, M. *Being Human: The Problem of Agency.* Cambridge University Press, 2000

[2] Berger, P., & Luckmann, T. *The Social Construction of Reality.* Anchor Books, 1966

interference), offering a suggestive parallel to the model's informational ontology.[1] Agency becomes **relational**, embedded in structures that both constrain and enable action.

7.7 Implications

This synthesis has several implications:

- **For Science:** It challenges strict reductionism, encouraging dialogue between physics, information theory, cognitive science, and phenomenology.
- **For Philosophy:** It reframes ontology as **interactive** rather than static, foregrounding the interface of structure and participation.
- **For Cosmology:** It suggests that observable reality may be **localised** within a broader informational continuum, re-opening questions about the **transcendence** of the soul and the scope of participatory agency.

Taken together, the model affirms that what '*is*' cannot be fully separated from how it becomes **known, enacted, and co-created**.

[1] Busemeyer, J. R., & Wang, Z. "Quantum cognition: Modeling behavior in entangled contexts." *Current Directions in Psychological Science* 24, no. 6 (2015): 442–448

CHAPTER 8

CONCLUSION

8.1 Summary of Findings

This monograph set out to confront one of the most enduring questions in both philosophical and scientific discourse: *What is reality?* The preceding chapters developed a model that integrates physical, metaphysical, temporal, and quantum-informational structures, culminating in a participatory ontology in which consciousness and the soul phenomenon play indispensable roles. This chapter synthesises those findings by drawing together the conceptual threads that emerged across the earlier analyses.

The central achievement of this work is the articulation of the **Multi-Dimensional Causational Model**, an ontology in which the **Physical**, **Metaphysical**, and **Temporal** dimensions interlock to form the foundational structure of reality. These dimensions operate within a deeper **Quantum Substrate**, the probabilistic informational matrix through which coherence, entanglement, and potentiality give rise to the structural and causal contours of the universe. Entropy introduces directionality and asymmetry into this structure, ensuring that time unfolds irreversibly and that every conscious act reshapes the range of possible futures[1].

Yet structure alone is insufficient to explain actuality. The monograph therefore incorporated **consciousness** as a participatory agent, arguing that it cannot be reduced to the merely emergent properties of neural complexity. Rather, consciousness stands at the interface of potentiality and actuality, exercising a subtle but real causal influence upon quantum-informational states[2]. In accepting this, the model positions consciousness not as a passive witness of physical events but as an active collaborator in the ongoing becoming of reality. This view is consonant with participatory interpretations of quantum mechanics, including Wheeler's proposal that the universe is brought into determinate form through acts of observation[3].

A third contribution concerns the **soul phenomenon**, conceived as the underlying substrate of

[1] Carroll, Sean. *From Eternity to Here: The Quest for the Ultimate Theory of Time*. New York: Dutton, 2010

[2] David J. Chalmers. The Conscious Mind: In Search of a Fundamental Theory. Oxford University Press, 1996

[3] John Archibald Wheeler. "Law Without Law." In Quantum Theory and Measurement, edited by J. A. Wheeler and W. H. Zurek, Princeton University Press, 1983

informational continuity and agency. The monograph considered two plausible ontological trajectories.

- **Option A** framed the soul as a **quantum-informational field** internal to this universe, capable of sustaining coherence while nonetheless subject to entropic limits[1].
- **Option B** suggested a **transcendent** soul, potentially persisting across cosmological cycles or multiversal frameworks, rooted in deeper informational structures beyond spacetime[2].

While both options remain speculative, each offers a conceptual pathway for understanding identity, continuity, and agency beyond physical dissolution.

The final extension of the model moved from the individual to the collective scale. Civilizations were construed as **metaphysical fields**, constituted by shared meanings, symbolic forms, and institutional architectures. These fields shape collective probability cones that widen or narrow depending on metaphysical coherence. When meaning collapses, collective agency contracts; when meaning stabilises, civilizations

[1] Roger Penrose. Shadows of the Mind: A Search for the Missing Science of Consciousness. Oxford University Press, 1994

[2] Max Tegmark. Our Mathematical Universe: My Quest for the Ultimate Nature of Reality. Knopf, 2014

flourish. The result is an integrated model in which individual agency and civilizational trajectories share a common causational architecture.

Together, these findings form a coherent ontological synthesis: reality is neither fixed nor fragmentary, but a **participatory continuum** in which structure and consciousness codetermine what becomes actual.

8.2 Implications

The implications of this synthesis span scientific, philosophical, civilizational, and cosmological domains. Each implication reinforces the central insight that reality emerges from the interplay of structural dimensions and conscious participation.

Scientific Implications

The model challenges exclusively reductionist accounts of reality by emphasising the limitations of purely classical frameworks. In particular, it questions whether classical physicalism can adequately address subjective experience, observer-dependent features of quantum measurement, and the unity of consciousness. The participatory role of consciousness, while speculative, encourages interdisciplinary exploration of quantum-biological processes, informational theories of physics, and non-classical explanations of cognition[1,2,3]. If consciousness participates in the collapse or selection of quantum-informational states, then scientific inquiry must broaden its methodological horizon beyond third-person empiricism.

Philosophical Implications

Philosophically, the model advances a relational and participatory ontology. It synthesises insights from phenomenology, information theory, and cosmology to argue that reality is not wholly objective nor wholly subjective but emerges at the interface where meaning meets structure. Experience is thus not a bystander in the universe's unfolding but one of its constitutive elements. This reframes fundamental questions concerning ontology, epistemology, and identity. Meaning becomes a causal variable; agency becomes structurally embedded; and the soul phenomenon becomes a legitimate topic of ontological inquiry rather than a remnant of pre-scientific metaphysics.

[1] Roger Penrose. Shadows of the Mind: A Search for the Missing Science of Consciousness. Oxford University Press, 199

[2] Max Tegmark. Our Mathematical Universe: My Quest for the Ultimate Nature of Reality. Knopf, 2014

[3] Giulio Tononi. "Consciousness as Integrated Information: A Provisional Manifesto." Biological Bulletin 215, no. 3 (2008): 216–242

Civilizational and Ethical Implications

At the collective scale, the model reveals that civilizations depend not merely on material resources but on **coherent metaphysical frameworks**. Shared meaning, moral orientation, institutional trust, and symbolic stability widen a society's probability cone, enabling resilience, innovation, and flourishing. Conversely, fragmentation of meaning produces negation-aligned agency—narrowing civilizational futures and increasing fragility. Ethical responsibility thus extends beyond individual conduct to the maintenance and renewal of the metaphysical fields that sustain collective life. Civilizational decline, in this view, is not merely historical contingency but a structural consequence of metaphysical disintegration.

Cosmological Implications

Cosmologically, the model opens onto deeper possibilities. If reality is informationally grounded, and if consciousness plays a participatory role in its unfolding, then the observable universe may be only one region within a broader ontological landscape. Option B's transcendent soul raises questions about continuity across cosmological cycles, multiversal horizons, or informational fields beyond spacetime. Even under Option A, which confines the soul to this universe, consciousness remains central to the emergence of actuality. In either case, the cosmos is not an indifferent expanse but a participatory field in which agency and meaning play real roles.

8.3 Limitations

This monograph acknowledges the **speculative** character of several core proposals. Empirical evidence for quantum-level contributions to consciousness remains contested, and no current experimental framework conclusively demonstrates that conscious observation collapses quantum states. While suggestive research exists in quantum biology and microtubule function[1][2][3][4][5], such findings remain preliminary and open to alternative interpretations.

[1] Hameroff, Stuart, and Roger Penrose. "Consciousness in the Universe: A Review of the 'Orch OR' Theory." Physics of Life Reviews 11, no. 1 (2014): 39–78

[2] Penrose, Roger. Shadows of the Mind: A Search for the Missing Science of Consciousness. Oxford: Oxford University Press, 1994

[3] Al-Khalili, Jim, and Johnjoe McFadden. Life on the Edge: The Coming Age of Quantum Biology. New York: Crown, 2014

[4] Craddock, Travis J. A., et al. "Anesthetic Alterations of Collective Terahertz Oscillations in Tubulin Correlate with Clinical Potency." Scientific Reports 7 (2017): 9877

[5] Engel, Greg S., et al. "Evidence for Wavelike Energy Transfer in Photosynthesis." Nature 446, no. 7137 (2007): 782–786

Methodologically, combining phenomenology, metaphysics, quantum theory, neuroscience, and civilizational analysis risks producing category errors or conceptual tensions. The dual framing of consciousness as both emergent and participatory may require further refinement to avoid incoherence. Similarly, the use of "soul" as a term carries unavoidable cultural and theological connotations. Although deployed here in a strictly ontological sense, readers may interpret it through inherited frameworks the monograph does not endorse.

Additionally, the symbolic and mathematical formulations presented in Chapters 3 and 6 are heuristic rather than predictive. They serve to clarify relational structure but do not constitute formal physical theories. This limitation is not a flaw but an acknowledgement of scope: the monograph aims to **theorise possibilities**, not to establish empirically verifiable laws.

8.4 Future Research Directions

The multi-dimensional causational model advanced in this monograph opens several avenues for empirical, theoretical, and philosophical exploration. Each direction arises organically from the synthesis of physical, metaphysical, temporal, and quantum-informational dimensions, and each is shaped by the participatory ontology that positions consciousness and the soul phenomenon as active contributors to actuality.

First, future research must engage more deeply with emerging work in **quantum biology**, particularly in the study of **coherence**, **entanglement**, and **microtubular quantum processes**, all of which provide suggestive—though not conclusive—evidence for quantum-level contributions to conscious states[1]. These empirical domains offer a promising foundation for assessing whether consciousness interacts with quantum informational structures in ways consistent with the participatory model, or whether more classical explanations suffice. A rigorous empirical program should therefore test the plausibility of nonclassical informational substrates, especially those implicated in the Orch-OR proposal[2] and in studies of anesthetic action on microtubular dynamics[3].

Second, **cosmological modelling** constitutes another major frontier. The consideration of **cyclic cosmologies**, **multiverse frameworks**, and **low-entropy**

[1] Hameroff, Stuart, and Roger Penrose. "Consciousness in the Universe: A Review of the 'Orch OR' Theory." Physics of Life Reviews 11, no. 1 (2014): 39–78

[2] Penrose, Roger. Shadows of the Mind: A Search for the Missing Science of Consciousness. Oxford: Oxford University Press, 1994

[3] Craddock, Travis J. A., et al. "Anesthetic Alterations of Collective Terahertz Oscillations in Tubulin Correlate with Clinical Potency." Scientific Reports 7 (2017): 9877

boundary conditions raises profound questions regarding informational continuity across cosmological horizons[1]. If the soul phenomenon operates as a quantum-informational substrate, then its potential persistence beyond physical dissolution cannot be fully assessed without corresponding cosmological inquiry. Theoretical models of pre-spacetime informational fields, vacuum fluctuations, and entropy dynamics may yield insights into whether continuity is intracosmic, as in Option A, or transcosmic, as suggested in Option B[2].

Third, ongoing **philosophical inquiry** is essential for refining the relational and participatory ontology developed in this work. This model builds upon phenomenology, social ontology, information theory, and metaphysics, each of which contributes distinct conceptual tools. However, integrating these traditions raises methodological challenges that call for greater philosophical precision. Future work must clarify the conceptual status of consciousness as both emergent and participatory, articulate the ontological standing of the soul without collapsing into theological categories, and refine the conceptual boundaries

[1] Smolin, Lee. The Life of the Cosmos. Oxford: Oxford University Press, 1997

[2] Tegmark, Max. Our Mathematical Universe: My Quest for the Ultimate Nature of Reality. New York: Knopf, 2014

between structural explanation and participatory agency[1].

Finally, future research must explore the **ethical and existential implications** of the participatory model. If agency, meaning, and consciousness shape the probability landscape of both individual and civilizational futures, then the cultivation of metaphysical coherence becomes a moral responsibility. This direction entails interdisciplinary collaboration between ethics, political philosophy, cultural theory, and civilizational modelling. Understanding how metaphysical fields stabilize, fragment, or renew will be crucial for assessing the future trajectories of advanced societies[2].

8.5 Closing Reflection

The participatory ontology articulated in this monograph reframes one of humanity's oldest questions: *What is reality?* The preceding chapters have argued that reality is not a passive backdrop, but a dynamic continuum shaped by structural conditions and activated by conscious participation. Classical physics, quantum theory, phenomenology, and social

[1] Thompson, Evan. Mind in Life: Biology, Phenomenology, and the Sciences of Mind. Cambridge, MA: Harvard University Press, 2007

[2] Thompson, Evan. Mind in Life: Biology, Phenomenology, and the Sciences of Mind. Cambridge, MA: Harvard University Press, 2007

ontology each contribute indispensable insights, but none is sufficient on its own. Only when these perspectives are integrated can reality be understood as an interface—dynamic, relational, and meaning-laden—between potentiality and actuality.

Within this framework, **consciousness** is not merely an epiphenomenon of neural complexity but a constitutive element of how reality becomes determinate. Observation is not synonymous with measurement; rather, consciousness participates in the actualisation of informational potential, shaping which among many possible futures becomes real[1]. This participatory role does not violate physical lawfulness but expresses an ontological depth that classical frameworks leave unaddressed. In this sense, the human person is a self-correcting causational circuit: agency is never terminal, meaning is never final, and reality is continuously co-created through recursive participation.

Likewise, the **soul phenomenon** emerges as a pivotal concept. Though speculative, the soul—conceived as a quantum-informational substrate that sustains coherence, identity, and agency over time—provides the missing interior axis through which consciousness

[1] Wheeler, John Archibald. "Law Without Law." In Quantum Theory and Measurement, edited by John A. Wheeler and Wojciech H. Zurek, 182–213. Princeton: Princeton University Press, 1983

exerts continuity across the entropic progression of life[1]. Whether this substrate is confined to this universe or participates in a deeper informational continuum, its role within the model is to anchor the agent within the multi-dimensional field of causation.

Ultimately, the participatory model affirms that knowing, acting, and perceiving are themselves causational. Every conscious act is not merely a response to reality but a contribution to its unfolding. The cosmos does not stand apart from its witnesses; it becomes through participation. This insight, though resonant with ancient metaphysical traditions, gains new vitality when articulated through the conceptual resources of modern physics, information theory, and phenomenological philosophy.

8.6 Limitations and Speculative Nature

The model developed in this monograph is intentionally integrative, but such integration entails significant limitations. Foremost, the proposed quantum-informational grounding of consciousness remains empirically underdetermined. Although quantum biological phenomena—such as coherence in photosynthesis, avian magnetoreception, and microtubular

[1] Penrose, Roger. Shadows of the Mind. Oxford: Oxford University Press, 199

dynamics—are increasingly well-documented[1], their relevance to consciousness remains contested. No current experimental framework conclusively demonstrates that conscious intention collapses quantum states, nor that the soul exists as a measurable substrate. The Orch-OR theory, while suggestive, has not achieved broad consensus within neuroscience or physics[2].

Further, combining phenomenology, metaphysics, social ontology, neuroscience, and quantum theory risks conflating heterogeneous methodologies. The participatory model walks a conceptual tightrope in portraying consciousness as both emergent and fundamental. Without careful refinement, this duality may invite charges of inconsistency. Similarly, the terminology of "soul," while employed here in a strictly ontological sense, carries historical and theological associations that could obscure the intended philosophical meaning[3].

Next, the symbolic and mathematical formulations presented earlier are **heuristic** rather than predictive. They clarify relational structure but do not attempt to model empirical processes in a testable way. This limitation is not a flaw but a reflection of the monograph's

[1] Al-Khalili, Jim, and Johnjoe McFadden. Life on the Edge: The Coming Age of Quantum Biology. New York: Crown, 2014

[2] Tegmark, Max. "Importance of Quantum Decoherence in Brain Processes." Physical Review E 61, no. 4 (2000): 4194–420

[3] MacIntyre, Alasdair. Dependent Rational Animals: Why Human Beings Need the Virtues. Chicago: Open Court, 1999

scope: to articulate a comprehensive ontology rather than a physical theory. Nevertheless, some readers may find the lack of formal testability a constraint on the model's scientific ambitions[1].

Finally, the speculative dimension of Options A and B—regarding whether the soul's informational substrate is intracosmic or transcosmic—must be acknowledged explicitly. These hypotheses are conceptual tools, not empirical claims. Their function is to illuminate ontological possibilities and to frame questions that future science and philosophy might explore[2].

8.7 The Participatory Cosmos

In concluding this synthesis, the model affirms a vision of reality that is simultaneously scientific and existential. Reality is not a silent stage, but a continuum brought into being through conscious participation. Every act of perception collapses potentiality into actuality; every intention alters the configuration of probabilistic futures; every choice generates ripples across the multi-dimensional field of causation[3].

[1] Meadows, Donella H. Thinking in Systems: A Primer. White River Junction, VT: Chelsea Green, 2008

[2] Deutsch, David. The Fabric of Reality: The Science of Parallel Universes—and Its Implications. London: Penguin, 1997

[3] Stapp, Henry P. Mindful Universe: Quantum Mechanics and the Participating Observer. Berlin: Springer, 2007

If consciousness is the soul's active expression—its interface with the physical, metaphysical, temporal, and quantum dimensions—then human agency becomes the existential engine through which the cosmos realises itself[1]. Without perception, the universe is mute; without interpretation, it is without meaning; without participation, it remains suspended in potentiality. In this light, humanity is not peripheral but central: the participatory axis through which meaning enters the world.

This is not anthropocentrism but ontological recognition. The cosmos, vast and intricate, may depend upon conscious agents to render its potential intelligible and actual. The stars shine, galaxies turn, entropy rises, but these phenomena become *real for us* only through the interpretive and participatory structure of consciousness[2]. The universe unfolds through us because we are the agents through whom meaning becomes manifest.

Thus, the participatory cosmos is not a metaphor but an ontological insight. Reality is co-created, not discovered; lived, not merely observed. To act, to choose, to perceive is to participate in the becoming

[1] Chalmers, David J. The Conscious Mind: In Search of a Fundamental Theory. New York: Oxford University Press, 1996

[2] Merleau-Ponty, Maurice. Phenomenology of Perception. London: Routledge, 1962

of the universe. In this sense, the soul phenomenon—conceived as continuity of agency and informational coherence—is not a speculative addendum but the deepest expression of what it means for the cosmos to know itself.

APPENDIX A
MATHEMATICAL FOUNDATIONS

A.1 Introduction

This appendix outlines the mathematical and symbolic scaffolding that supports the **Multi-Dimensional Causational Model**. The formulations here are not intended as experimentally validated physics but as **conceptual mathematics**—symbolic structures that clarify relationships between the physical, metaphysical, temporal, and quantum dimensions of reality. The emphasis is on **intuition, structure, and coherence**, not on empirical prediction.

The mathematical and symbolic formulations presented in this appendix function as conceptual scaffolding rather than predictive models. They are intended to clarify structural relationships within the multidimensional causational framework, not to assert empirical equivalence with physical quantum systems.

A.2 Dimensional State Representation

Let:

- **P(t)** = Physical Reality at time *t*
- **M(t)** = Metaphysical Reality at time *t*
- **T(t)** = Temporal (entropic) structure at time *t*
- **Q(t)** = Quantum informational substrate at time *t*
- **C(t)** = Consciousness / Soul phenomenon at time *t*

Then:
$R(t) = f(P(t), M(t), T(t), Q(t), C(t))$
This expression represents the **experienced reality state** at any moment. Each dimension contributes a component of causation.

A.3 Entropic Constraint and Arrow of Time

Entropy imposes a monotonic constraint: $\frac{dS}{dt} \geq 0$

This constraint applies at the level of closed systems or the universe as a whole; local subsystems may temporarily decrease entropy by exporting it. The condition therefore encodes the global arrow of time rather than local monotonicity.

Where **S** is entropy. This generates:

- irreversibility
- causational directionality
- temporal horizons
- "narrowing" of probability cones without intervention

In metaphysical and civilizational contexts, entropy analogues include:

- breakdown of coherence
- fragmentation of meaning
- institutional decay

A.4 Quantum-Informational Layer

Reality's quantum substrate **Q** is modelled as a probability distribution or density operator:

$$\rho(t) \in HP \otimes HM \otimes H_Q$$

These Hilbert spaces function as abstract informational state spaces rather than literal quantum physical fields. The notation provides a formal idiom for contextuality, updating, and probabilistic reweighting without implying that metaphysical structures possess quantum physical properties.

The state updates through an **intervention operator** E representing physical, metaphysical, or agentive events:

$$\rho(t + 1) = E\rho(t)$$

The probability of specific outcomes:

$$P(\text{future state}) = \mathrm{Tr}(\Pi\rho(t + 1))$$

Where **Π** is a projector representing a potential actual outcome.

A.5 Potentiality to Actuality Transition

The transition from quantum potentiality to actuality is schematically expressed as:

$$\psi \rightarrow |\psi\_{i}\rangle$$

where $C(t)$—the consciousness/soul phenomenon—plays a participatory role in selecting among admissible outcomes.

This is **not** a claim of physical collapse by consciousness, but an **ontological framing** in which consciousness participates in how actuality becomes meaningful and coherent.

A.5.1 Recursive Participatory Feedback

Because participation is not terminal, realised outcomes feed back into both consciousness and metaphysical structure. Let R(t) denote the realised reality state following actualisation. Then:

$$C(t + 1) = g(C(t), R(t))$$
$$M(t + 1) = h(M(t), R(t))$$

where *g*and *h*represent interpretive and integrative processes through which experience revises identity, meaning, and future agency.

This recursive structure encodes the self-correcting character of agency: action actualises potentiality, consequence returns as experience, and subsequent participation is re-weighted accordingly. The system therefore forms a closed but non-static causational circuit rather than a linear chain of effects.

A.6 Probability Cones and Causational Geometry

A **probability cone** expresses how future pathways widen or narrow over time.

Let **Ω(t)** represent the set of viable future states at time t.

Then:

- Widening cone: $|\Omega(t + 1)| > |\Omega(t)|$
- Narrowing cone: $|\Omega(t + 1)| < |\Omega(t)|$

Metaphysical coherence tends to widen cones. Entropy and meaning-collapse tend to narrow them.

A.7 Life-Cone Geometry

Each individual's life trajectory is modelled as a **cone** widening from conception and tapering along the entropic axis. Let:

- **r(t)** = radius of influence (physical + metaphysical)
- **z(t)** = temporal progression

The cone shape reflects:

- growth → expansion
- stabilisation → plateau
- entropic taper → narrowing

Multiple cones superimpose into a **civilizational field**, creating collective futures.

A.8 Soul Continuity (Informational Substrate)

Two mathematically expressible possibilities:
Option A — Finite, Intracosmic Continuity
The soul function **C(t)** decays as coherence diminishes:

$$C(t) \propto e^{-\lambda t}$$

where λ represents decoherence.

Option B — Transcendent Continuity

The soul substrate exists over an expanded domain:

$$C\infty(t) \notin HP \quad \text{but} \quad C\infty \in Hmeta$$

representing continuity beyond spacetime.

APPENDIX B
FIGURES AND DIAGRAMS

B.1 Diagram 1 — Multi-Dimensional Causational Model

Diagram 1 depicts the model's architecture: the Physical, Metaphysical, and Temporal dimensions rest upon the Quantum Substrate, while the Reality Interface Layer mediates A layered schematic showing:

- Base: **Quantum Substrate**
- Above: **Physical**, **Metaphysical**, **Temporal** dimensions
- Upper layer: **Reality Interface Layer**
- Top arc: **Consciousness**

Information flows upward from potentiality → structure → experiential actualisation.

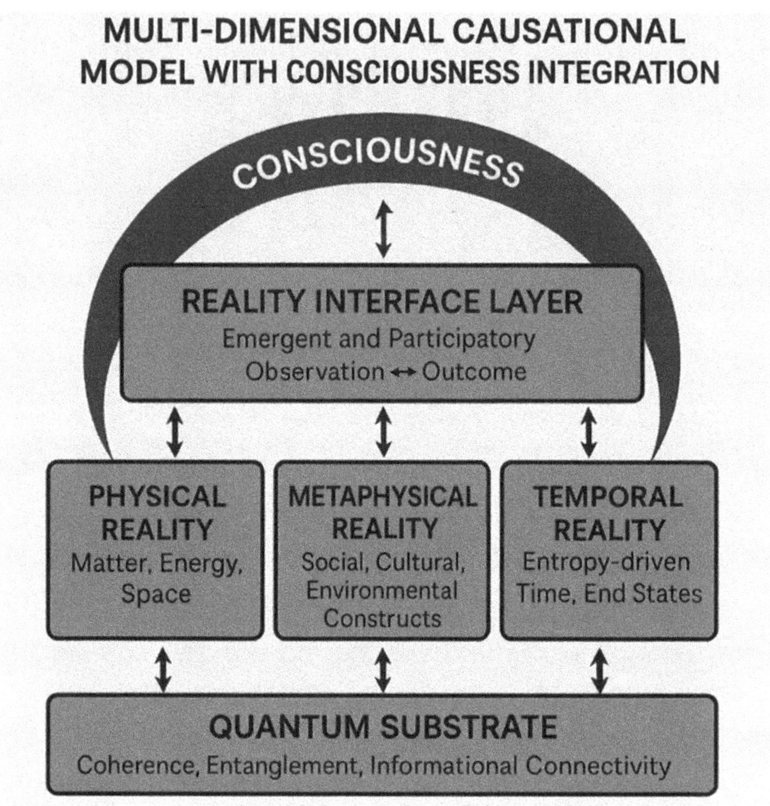

B.2 Figure 2 — Growth and Endurance of the Soul

Figure 2 visualises a **single life-cone**. Originating at a luminous node (physical conception), the cone widens rapidly (growth and maximal potential) before tapering along the entropic time axis. A vertical plane marks the **present**, locally instantiating the model of Diagram 1. A faint continuation beyond the cone's tip gestures to the **possible endurance** of the soul phenomenon beyond physical death. Along this trajectory, the agent repeatedly crosses the reality interface: action actualises potential, consequence returns as experience, and identity is recursively revised rather than progressing in a single linear direction. The image is not empirical evidence but a conceptual aid to think **continuity**, **agency**, and **trajectory**.

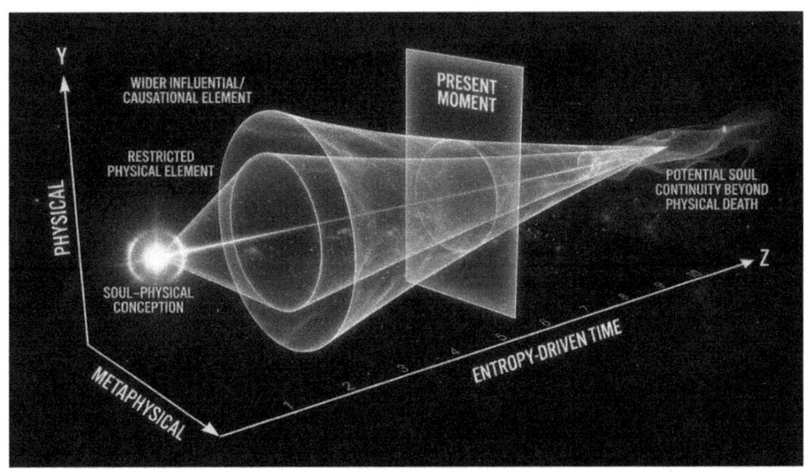

Figure 2 - Growth and Endurance of the Soul Phenomenon

A 3-axis cone diagram:

- **X-axis**: Metaphysical dimension
- **Y-axis**: Physical dimension
- **Z-axis**: Entropic time
- Bright node = conception

- Cone widens (development)
- Cone tapers (entropy, ageing)
- A faint extension beyond lifespan represents hypothetical soul continuity.

B.3 Figure 3 — Multiple Life Cones Across Entropic Time

Figure 3 extends the cone-grid to a **block-time** perspective, with multiple life-cones embedded within shared metaphysical, physical, and entropic coordinates. Overlapping cones highlight **collective influence** and **co-creation**: a single cone models individual agency; a cluster shows how interacting agents can reshape the metaphysical environment. Each cone represents not a fixed path but a series of recursive interface crossings, where collective and individual actions generate consequences that return as shared experience, reshaping future possibilities. The vertical plane labelled **"Present Moment"** intersects all cones, underscoring that actuality is always realised **together**, across persons and time.

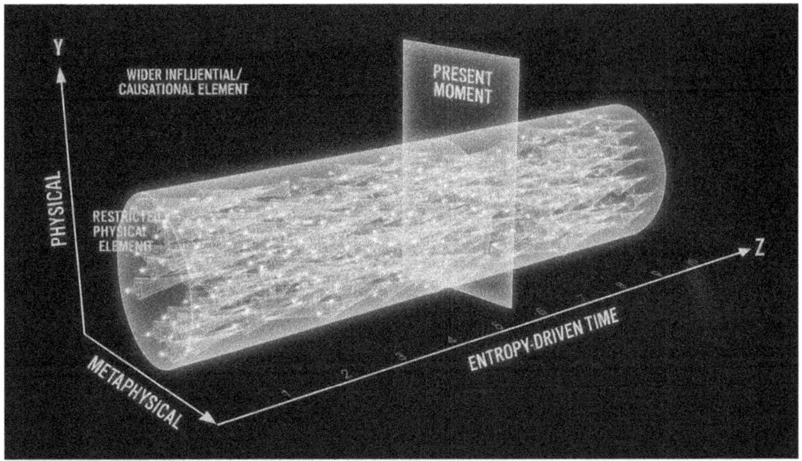

Figure 3 - Potential Influence of Multiple Life Cones on Reality

A cylindrical block-time space where many life-cones overlap:

- **Each cone** = an individual trajectory
- Overlaps show shared structures, institutions, meaning systems
- **Vertical plane** = the "present moment" across all agents
- Convergence/divergence patterns illustrate civilizational coherence or fragmentation
- Cylindrical blue halo = Civilizational/causational field/shield.

B.4 Figure 4 — The Recursive Participatory Agent

Figure 4 — The Recursive Participatory Agent. Identity, meaning, and agency are continuously revised through repeated crossings of the reality interface, where potentiality is actualised and returns as experienced consequence within a self-correcting causational circuit.

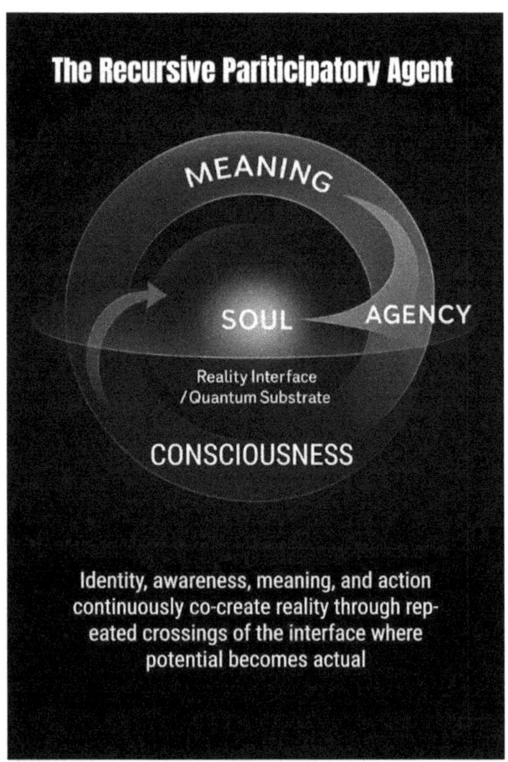

Figure 4 – The Recursive Participatory Agent

APPENDIX C
GLOSSARY OF TECHNICAL AND PHILOSOPHICAL TERMS

A complete glossary for the monograph ***Reality as a Multi-Dimensional Causational Field.***

Foundational Ontological Terms

1. **Actuality**
   The realised state of events once potentiality collapses into determinate form.
2. **Agency**
   The capacity of an individual or collective to influence outcomes through intention and action.
3. **Arrow of Time**
   The directionality of temporal progression, grounded in entropy's irreversible increase.
4. **Being-in-the-World**
   A phenomenological term emphasising lived, situated experience rather than detached observation.

5. **Boundary Condition**
   A constraint that shapes the behaviour or evolution of a system (e.g., low-entropy initial state).
6. **Causation (Classical)**
   Linear, law-governed relationships between cause and effect in physical systems.
7. **Causation (Quantum)**
   Probabilistic and contextual influence among quantum states, lacking strict determinism.
8. **Causational Field**
   The integrated environment where physical, meta-physical, temporal, and informational influences interact.
9. **Causal Graph**
   A structured map of variables and their directional influences within a system.
10. **Coherence (Metaphysical)**
    The stability and clarity of shared meanings, norms, and identity structures.

Model-Specific Terminology

11. **Cone-Grid**
    The geometric arrangement of Life-Cones across entropic time.
12. **Consciousness (Participatory)**
    The phenomenon that both perceives reality and contributes to its actualisation.

13. **Continuity (Soul)**
    The persistent informational identity that endures across temporal intervals.
14. **Creation-Aligned Agency**
    Forms of action that widen probability cones, enhance coherence, and generate futures.
15. **Decoherence**
    The process by which quantum systems lose coherent informational states and become classical.
16. **Dimension (Physical)**
    The structural domain of matter, energy, and space.
17. **Dimension (Metaphysical)**
    The symbolic and cultural matrix that shapes meaning and interpretation.
18. **Dimension (Temporal)**
    The axis structured by entropy and irreversibility.
19. **Emergence**
    The arising of higher-order properties from lower-level structures.
20. **Entanglement**
    Quantum correlations between particles or states that behave as unified wholes.

Quantum and Informational Terms

21. **Eigenstate**
    A definite state resulting after a quantum measurement.

22. **Hilbert Space**
    The mathematical structure representing all possible states of a system.
23. **Information (Quantum)**
    A primitive component of reality representing distinctions encoded in physical or metaphysical states.
24. **Intervention Operator (E)**
    A transformation that updates the state of the system.
25. **Measurement (Quantum)**
    The act that yields a specific outcome from superposed potentialities.
26. **Microtubule**
    A cellular structure hypothesised to support quantum informational processes.
27. **Nonlocality**
    The capacity for instantaneous correlations across spatial separation.
28. **Objective Reduction (OR)**
    A proposed mechanism for state collapse driven by gravitational thresholds.
29. **Potentiality**
    The realm of unactualised but possible states.
30. **Quantum Substrate**
    The informational foundation enabling coherence, superposition, and probabilistic structure.

Temporal and Entropic Terms

31. **Entropy (Physical)**
    A measure of disorder or the dispersal of energy.
32. **Entropy (Civilizational)**
    The drift toward fragmentation of meaning and institutional instability.
33. **End-State**
    The terminal condition toward which an entropic system evolves.
34. **Entropic Time**
    Time's irreversible direction linked to the second law of thermodynamics.
35. **Future Cone**
    The geometry of possible futures available at a given moment.
36. **Heat Death**
    A hypothetical cosmic end-state with maximal entropy and no usable energy.
37. **Irreversibility**
    The property of processes that cannot be undone.
38. **Low-Entropy Origin**
    The highly ordered state of the early universe.
39. **Temporal Horizon**
    The limit beyond which prediction or influence is constrained.

40. **Trajectory (Causational)**
    The path a system or agent follows through entropic time.

Phenomenological and Philosophical Terms

41. **Actualisation**
    The bringing-forth of a determinate state through participation or observation.
42. **Attunement**
    The alignment between inner consciousness and outer world-structure.
43. **Embodiment**
    The grounding of consciousness within physical structures.
44. **Epistemological Relationalism**
    The position that knowledge arises from interpretative relationships, not from raw data.
45. **Existential Orientation**
    A person's deep interpretive stance toward meaning, value, and action.
46. **Hermeneutics**
    The study of interpretation and meaning-making.
47. **Intentionality**
    The directedness of consciousness toward objects or meanings.

48. **Interpretive Horizon**
    The background of assumptions that shapes how reality is perceived.
49. **Metaphysical Coherence**
    The internal alignment of symbolic, ethical, and narrative structures.
50. **Normativity**
    The dimension of value, obligation, and what "ought" to be.

Soul and Consciousness Terms

51. **Agency Field**
    The sphere in which intentional actions exert influence.
52. **Attentional Collapse**
    The focusing of consciousness that contributes to state reduction.
53. **Continuity Substrate**
    The underlying informational structure preserving identity.
54. **Interior Axis**
    The internal center through which meaning and agency are unified.
55. **Locative Identity**
    The placement of self within a metaphysical and historical context.

56. **Moral Orientation**
    The direction of agency according to values or meaning.
57. **Participatory Agent**
    A consciousness capable of influencing the unfolding of actuality.
58. **Preconscious Interface**
    The sub-threshold domain where probabilistic structures reorganize before awareness.
59. **Soul (Informational)**
    The non-material substrate that stores coherence across time.
60. **Transcendent Continuity**
    A form of persistence not bound strictly by this universe's parameters.

Civilizational and Collective Terms

61. **Civilizational Field**
    The metaphysical environment shaped by shared narratives and institutions.
62. **Civilizational Probability Cone**
    The range of futures available to a culture or society.
63. **Collective Agency**
    The aggregated influence of many agents acting within shared meaning structures.

64. **Collective Actualisation**
The emergence of shared outcomes through joint participation.
65. **Collective Consciousness**
The distributed awareness embodied in cultural and institutional forms.
66. **Cultural Entropy**
The breakdown of cohesive narratives and moral orientation.
67. **Expressive Individualism**
A mode of selfhood centered on inner authenticity over shared values.
68. **Institutional Coherence**
The degree to which institutions align with cultural and metaphysical structures.
69. **Meaning Architecture**
The framework of values, stories, and practices that stabilise a society.
70. **Negation-Aligned Agency**
Action patterns that erode coherence and narrow future possibilities.

Mathematical and Formal Terms

71. **Density Operator (ρ)**
A mathematical representation of the state of a system.

72. **Diagonalisation**
    The transformation of a matrix to reveal its eigenstructure.
73. **Domain (State Space)**
    The set of all possible states a system may occupy.
74. **Exponential Decay**
    A function describing diminishing coherence in intracosmic continuity.
75. **Hilbert Tensor Product**
    The combination of multiple state spaces into a unified configuration.
76. **Interventionist Causality**
    The study of how deliberate actions change outcome distributions.
77. **Operator (Quantum)**
    A mathematical object that transforms states.
78. **Probability Distribution**
    A mathematical function describing possible outcomes.
79. **Projector (Π)**
    A measurement operator selecting particular outcomes.
80. **State Space**
    The entirety of potential states a system could inhabit.

Metaphysical and Narrative Terms

81. **Anchoring Narrative**
    A story or symbol that stabilizes meaning within a culture.
82. **Civilizational Horizon**
    The outer boundary of a society's imagined possibilities.
83. **Cocreation**
    The joint shaping of reality through multiple agents.
84. **Dialogical Identity**
    Identity formed through relationships and shared meaning.
85. **Endurance (Soul)**
    Persistence across entropic time.
86. **Identity Structure**
    The pattern of meanings and values that constitute a self.
87. **Metaphysical Gravity**
    The pull exerted by coherent meaning systems.
88. **Ontological Depth**
    The layered structure of reality beneath surface appearances.
89. **Participatory Cosmos**
    The idea that the universe becomes real through participation.

90. **Symbolic Form**
    Cultural structures—language, ritual, art—that mediate meaning.

Extended System Terms

91. **Adaptive Potential**
    The degree to which a system can respond to shifting conditions.
92. **Attractor State**
    A configuration toward which a system naturally evolves.
93. **Boundary Dissolution**
    The loss of differentiation between key metaphysical categories.
94. **Feedback Loop**
    A cyclical influence pattern amplifying or dampening effects.
95. **Horizon of Viability**
    The zone within which a system or society can continue to exist.
96. **Phase Transition**
    A sudden qualitative shift in system behaviour.
97. **Resonance (Metaphysical)**
    The amplifying effect of alignment between agents and meaning structures.

98. **Structural Constraint**
    A limit imposed by physical or metaphysical architecture.
99. **Systemic Fragility**
    Vulnerability to collapse due to weakened coherence.
100. **Topology of Meaning**
    The patterned distribution of metaphysical significance in a culture.

If you'd like:

✓ The glossary expanded to **150+ terms**
✓ Integration directly into your Appendices
✓ A .docx version automatically typeset
✓ Cross-links between glossary terms and chapter sections
✓ Glossary entries arranged into thematic clusters

BIBLIOGRAPHY

Philosophy, Metaphysics, and Ontology

Aristotle. *De Anima*. 350 BCE.

Berkeley, George. 1710. *A Treatise Concerning the Principles of Human Knowledge*.

Berger, Peter L., and Thomas Luckmann. 1966. *The Social Construction of Reality*. New York: Anchor Books.

Cassirer, Ernst. 1944. *An Essay on Man*. New Haven: Yale University Press.

Chalmers, David J. 1996. *The Conscious Mind: In Search of a Fundamental Theory*. Oxford: Oxford University Press.

Heidegger, Martin. 1962. *Being and Time*. New York: Harper & Row.

MacIntyre, Alasdair.

— 1981. *After Virtue*. Notre Dame: University of Notre Dame Press.

— 1999. *Dependent Rational Animals: Why Human Beings Need the Virtues*. Chicago: Open Court.

Merleau-Ponty, Maurice. 1962. *Phenomenology of Perception*. London: Routledge.

Popper, Karl. 1959. *The Logic of Scientific Discovery*. London: Routledge.

Psillos, Stathis. 1999. *Scientific Realism: How Science Tracks Truth*. London: Routledge.

Scheler, Max. 2009. *The Human Place in the Cosmos*. Evanston: Northwestern University Press.

Taylor, Charles. 1989. *Sources of the Self: The Making of the Modern Identity*. Cambridge: Harvard University Press.

Teilhard de Chardin, Pierre. 1955. *The Phenomenon of Man*. New York: Harper & Brothers.

Voegelin, Eric. 1952. *The New Science of Politics*. Chicago: University of Chicago Press.

Physics, Cosmology, Time, and Quantum Foundations

Bohr, Niels. 1949. "Discussion with Einstein on Epistemological Problems in Atomic Physics." In *Albert Einstein: Philosopher–Scientist*.

Carroll, Sean. 2010. *From Eternity to Here: The Quest for the Ultimate Theory of Time*. New York: Dutton.

Clausius, Rudolf. 1850. "On the Mechanical Theory of Heat." *Annalen der Physik*.

Davies, Paul. 1994. *The Last Three Minutes*. New York: Basic Books.

Engel, Greg S., et al. 2007. "Evidence for Wavelike Energy Transfer in Photosynthesis." *Nature* 446: 782–786.

Hawking, Stephen. 1988. *A Brief History of Time*. New York: Bantam Books.

Heisenberg, Werner. 1958. *Physics and Philosophy: The Revolution in Modern Science*. New York: Harper.

Newton, Isaac. 1687. *Philosophiæ Naturalis Principia Mathematica*.

Penrose, Roger.

— 1994. *Shadows of the Mind: A Search for the Missing Science of Consciousness*. Oxford: Oxford University Press.

— 2005. *The Road to Reality*. London: Vintage.

Smolin, Lee. 1997. *The Life of the Cosmos*. Oxford: Oxford University Press.

Steinhardt, Paul, and Neil Turok. 2002. "A Cyclic Model of the Universe." *Science* 296: 1436–1439.

Tegmark, Max.

— 2000. "Importance of Quantum Decoherence in Brain Processes." *Physical Review E* 61: 4194–4200.

— 2014. *Our Mathematical Universe: My Quest for the Ultimate Nature of Reality*. New York: Knopf.

Wheeler, John Archibald.

— 1983. "Law Without Law." In *Quantum Theory and Measurement*, ed. John A. Wheeler and Wojciech H. Zurek, 182–213. Princeton: Princeton University Press.

— 1990. "Information, Physics, Quantum: The Search for Links." In *Complexity, Entropy, and the Physics of Information*. Redwood City, CA: Addison-Wesley.

Consciousness, Neuroscience, and Quantum Mind

Craddock, Travis J. A., et al.

— 2015. "Anaesthetic Alterations of Microtubule Function Suggest a Role in Consciousness." *Frontiers in Psychology* 6: 1–12.

— 2015. "Anesthetics Act in Quantum Channels in Brain Microtubules to Prevent Consciousness." *Current Neuropharmacology* 15 (6): 523–533.

— 2017. "Anesthetic Alterations of Collective Terahertz Oscillations in Tubulin Correlate with Clinical Potency." *Scientific Reports* 7: 9877.

Edelman, Gerald. 1992. *Bright Air, Brilliant Fire: On the Matter of the Mind*. New York: Basic Books.

Hameroff, Stuart, and Roger Penrose. 2014. "Consciousness in the Universe: A Review of the Orch OR Theory." *Physics of Life Reviews* 11 (1): 39–78.

Lambert, Neill, Yuan-Chung Chen, Y-C. Cheng, C.-M. Li, G.-Y. Chen, and Franco Nori. 2013. "Quantum Biology." *Nature Physics* 9 (1): 10–18.

Libet, Benjamin. 1985. "Unconscious Cerebral Initiative and the Role of Conscious Will in Voluntary Action." *Behavioral and Brain Sciences* 8 (4): 529–566.

Tononi, Giulio. 2008. "Consciousness as Integrated Information: A Provisional Manifesto." *Biological Bulletin* 215 (3): 216–242.

Wigner, Eugene P. 1967. "Remarks on the Mind–Body

Question." In *Symmetries and Reflections*. Bloomington: Indiana University Press.

Al-Khalili, Jim, and Johnjoe McFadden. 2014. *Life on the Edge: The Coming Age of Quantum Biology*. New York: Crown.

Information Theory, Causality, and Quantum Cognition

Busemeyer, Jerome R., and Peter D. Bruza. 2012. *Quantum Models of Cognition and Decision*. Cambridge: Cambridge University Press.

Busemeyer, Jerome R., and Zheng Wang. 2015. "Quantum Cognition: Modeling Behavior in Entangled Contexts." *Current Directions in Psychological Science* 24 (6): 442–448.

Deutsch, David. 1997. *The Fabric of Reality: The Science of Parallel Universes—and Its Implications*. London: Penguin.

Leifer, Matthew S., and Robert W. Spekkens. 2013. "Towards a Formulation of Quantum Theory as a Causally Neutral Theory of Bayesian Inference." *Physical Review A* 88 (5): 052130.

Meadows, Donella H. 2008. *Thinking in Systems: A Primer*. White River Junction, VT: Chelsea Green.

Nielsen, Michael A., and Isaac L. Chuang. 2010. *Quantum Computation and Quantum Information*. Cambridge: Cambridge University Press.

Pearl, Judea. 2009. *Causality: Models, Reasoning, and Inference*. Cambridge: Cambridge University Press.

Reichenbach, Hans. 1956. *The Direction of Time*. Berkeley: University of California Press.

Stapp, Henry P. 2007. *Mindful Universe: Quantum Mechanics and the Participating Observer*. Berlin: Springer.

Civilizational Studies, Social Theory, Identity, and Agency

Archer, Margaret. 2000. *Being Human: The Problem of Agency*. Cambridge: Cambridge University Press.

Berger, Peter L., and Thomas Luckmann. 1966. *The Social Construction of Reality*. New York: Anchor Books.

Lasch, Christopher. 1979. *The Culture of Narcissism*. New York: W. W. Norton.

Taylor, Charles. 1989. *Sources of the Self: The Making of the Modern Identity*. Cambridge: Harvard University Press.

Voegelin, Eric. 1952. *The New Science of Politics*. Chicago: University of Chicago Press.

Teilhard de Chardin, Pierre. 1955. *The Phenomenon of Man*. New York: Harper & Brothers.

Thompson, Evan. 2007. *Mind in Life: Biology, Phenomenology, and the Sciences of Mind*. Cambridge, MA: Harvard University Press.

Fictional or Internal Works Referenced in the Monograph

Carlos, John R. 2026. *Cryonic Dreams: Awakening*. Silversmith Press.

www.ingramcontent.com/pod-product-compliance
Lightning Source LLC
LaVergne TN
LVHW052337100826
845147LV00020B/1096

* 9 7 8 1 9 6 7 3 8 6 5 7 4 *